# SINGLE GIRL PROBLEMS

# SINGLE GIRL PROBLEMS

WHY BEING
SINGLE ISN'T
A PROBLEM
TO BE SOLVED

## ANDREA BAIN

DUNDURN
TORONTO

Printer: Webcom
Back cover photo: David Grimes

**Library and Archives Canada Cataloguing in Publication**

Bain, Andrea, author
        Single girl problems : why being single isn't a problem to be solved
/ Andrea Bain.

Includes bibliographical references.
Issued in print and electronic formats.
ISBN 978-1-4597-3909-3 (softcover).--ISBN 978-1-4597-3910-9 (PDF).--
ISBN 978-1-4597-3911-6 (EPUB)

1. Single women--Social conditions--21st century. 2. Single women--
Conduct of life. 3. Single women. I. Title.

HQ800.2.B34 2018            306.81'53            C2017-906444-4

1    2    3    4    5        22    21        20    19    18

We acknowledge the support of the **Canada Council for the Arts**, which last year invested $153 million to bring the arts to Canadians throughout the country, and the **Ontario Arts Council** for our publishing program. We also acknowledge the financial support of the **Government of Ontario**, through the **Ontario Book Publishing Tax Credit** and the **Ontario Media Development Corporation**, and the **Government of Canada**.

Nous remercions le **Conseil des arts du Canada** de son soutien. L'an dernier, le Conseil a investi 153 millions de dollars pour mettre de l'art dans la vie des Canadiennes et des Canadiens de tout le pays.

Care has been taken to trace the ownership of copyright material used in this book. The author and the publisher welcome any information enabling them to rectify any references or credits in subsequent editions.
                                                                            — *J. Kirk Howard, President*

The publisher is not responsible for websites or their content unless they are owned by the publisher.

Printed and bound in Canada.

VISIT US AT

dundurn.com  |  @dundurnpress  |  dundurnpress  |  dundurnpress

Dundurn
3 Church Street, Suite 500
Toronto, Ontario, Canada
M5E 1M2

To my godmother,
Jean Pitt,
and all the other wonderful, intelligent,
beautiful single women around the world
whose love, support, inspiration,
and prayers have held me up and blessed me.
I dedicate this book to you.
I love you and thank you.

# CONTENTS

# INTRODUCTION

THERE IS NO RIGHT OR WRONG WAY to be single. There's also no guarantee that you will meet the love of your life by age 27, date for two years, then get engaged and be married by 30. What will most likely happen is you'll have a few crushes — in my case a lot of crushes. Some will like you back while others won't even know you're alive. Eventually you'll fall in love, which will feel so good I won't even bother trying to describe it to you. Some of your relationships will just fizzle, and some will break your heart into so many pieces that putting it back together will seem impossible.

At times you might be embarrassed to admit that you're still single because deep down you thought you would be married by now. Stop trying to explain to people why you're not. You don't owe them any answers. Conversely, never look at being single as a failure. Your life isn't about relationships but rather all the moments in between. Don't be afraid of your own company because no one can love you as much as you should love yourself. Loving yourself and learning to be self-sufficient are badges of honour — not only do they set the standard for how you want to be treated, but I believe these abilities give you the tools to be a better human being. Get to know who you are instead of waiting for some magical person to walk into your life and make you more adventurous, richer, nicer, smarter, sexier, or more relaxed in your own skin. That's too big a job for anyone to take on anyway. At the end of the day, all anyone wants to be is loved and appreciated, not burdened with your unresolved issues.

Being dumped is not the end of the world; instead, be thankful for the experience because you'll grow more from those uncomfortable moments than from any of the "nice" relationships. One of the most important gifts you'll receive as you get older is learning to listen and trust your inner voice — it's always right. If you're in tune with your gut and if you listen to your inner voice, you'll be able to tell when a relationship isn't working or know if the person you're dating is lying or cheating. And never let your desire to be in a relationship supersede your need to be happy.

Here's another very valuable piece of advice: no matter how cute that guy is, don't ever let him mistreat you or make you feel inferior. When you die no one will write the number of likes your Instagram photos got on your tombstone, so refrain from posting provocative pictures to get men to poke and double-tap. That attention is superficial. You are more than just your outward appearance; what's on the inside counts just as much — if not more. Lastly, if you ever get approached by a married man, pivot and run in the opposite direction.

These are all of the things I wish someone had told me before I started dating. Instead I had to learn these lessons through trial and error. I read a million self-help books and articles, watched every Oprah episode about relationships, studied and talked about relationships on television for over three years, and, most importantly, went to therapy before I put it all together.

A lot of this book is based on my experiences as a heterosexual woman trying to navigate the dating world in the twenty-first century, but my hope is that this book will empower, educate, and entertain gay, straight, trans, and bisexual people. That being said, I also know that I can't be everything to everyone.

Dating in the twenty-first century is nothing like it was 50 or so years ago. Back then things were simpler: people in their early 20s dated with the intention of getting married. It was the only way a girl could survive if she didn't want to live with her parents forever.

A woman's virtue was more important than her getting a diploma. Today the dating process is way more complex, and so are we. Women around the world in countries like Australia, Japan, Canada, India, and the United States are making major strides in the workforce, steadily climbing the corporate ladder, and breaking glass ceilings. The number of women in the highest paying jobs at the top 100 largest companies has doubled in the last 10 years, and attitudes toward women in leadership roles has changed for the better. At the same time, courtship has changed a lot as well. People are waiting longer to tie the knot, and technology has changed the playing field. Now there's online dating, texting instead of phone calls, dick pics, apps that help you break up with a person, and sliding into DMs. Even the dating language has changed. These seismic shifts in the twenty-first century have led many successful single women to ask, Is it possible to have it all? Are men intimidated by my achievements? Is it my destiny to spend the rest of my life alone?

Needless to say, this new dating era isn't for the weak. I liken it to riding an emotional roller coaster wearing a blindfold. One minute you're having the time of your life, and the next minute you don't know what the hell is going on and all you want to do is get off.

And I don't know if you've realized this yet, but everyone has baggage. Everyone! Anyone who tells you they don't have baggage is either a child or a damn liar. Between the crap our parents passed on to us and the double scoop of crap our exes put us through, it's a miracle some of us even leave the house. When it comes to dating, most of us feel about it the way my mother feels about technology — anxious, frustrated, and filled with hatred.

I remember my high school health class with Miss Good, who, God bless her heart, seemed just as anxious and inexperienced about sex as the awkward bunch of grade 9 students she was teaching. I always found it interesting how much importance was put on sex education, but nothing was ever said about dating and love. Now, I'm not dismissing the importance of sex education, but let's be real — it doesn't take a rocket scientist to figure out how to put tab A into slot B. My grandmother never had a class about her vulva, and she had 12 children. Homegirl figured it out! Relationships are way more complex, but for some reason our parents, friends, and society have always just assumed you'll pick the right person, settle down, get married, and push out a couple of kids. Easy, right? Grandma did that without any instructions. So when it doesn't happen the same way for you, those same people will chastise and blame you for not following the status quo. Why do people feel so comfortable attacking single people? I'll explore that question later on.

*Single Girl Problems* is a book that looks to change the narrative about what it means to be a single woman in the twenty-first century. We are driving the real estate market, running Fortune 500 companies, and having premarital sex. According to *New York Magazine*, single women are the most potent political force and are transforming American politics, so why are we still being treated like "spinsters" of the 1950s?

Getting married is still seen as a woman's biggest accomplishment — second only to becoming a mother. *Single Girl Problems* will help you see single life as an important journey to figure out who you are and what you want. If I achieve nothing else, I hope this book will reveal a more accurate picture of what it means to be single, help break down what's going on, and hopefully take a bit of the edge off. It's time to turn the page on the single woman's storyline.

# 1

# BEING SINGLE SUCKS

BEING SINGLE SUCKS! Well, that's what everyone tells me anyway. In pretty much every culture, single women over the age of 29 are seen as lonely, miserable, and undesirable crazy cat wranglers. Family members, friends, and heck, even my dentist, ask, "When are you going to get married?" And if one more person tells me about his third cousin twice removed who met the love of her life online, I'm going to take out my weave and eat it. I recently picked up my favourite magazine and was shocked to see that they had dedicated an entire issue to the "problem." Inside were detailed instructions for women on how to draw men out and hunt men down. Further instructions were provided on how to make him propose once you'd caught him in your trap. Very romantic — not! On the other side of the fence, the marketing department for married life is knocking it out of the park. Doesn't it look awesome? Married people go camping, eat dinner, ride bikes, and seem to have the time of their lives at the Sandals resort in Jamaica. The last time I saw a happy single woman in a television ad, she was marvelling at the absorbency of her new feminine hygiene product.

Seriously, take a look at how the media depicts single women. Let's start with one of our our poster girls, Bridget Jones. Bridget is a chubby, insecure, mid-level journalist who, in a Mr. Bean–like fashion, pursues two emotionally unavailable men while wearing, arguably, the most comfortable underwear. On the other end of the spectrum is Carrie Bradshaw, a freelance writer with impeccable fashion sense, great hair, three amazing friends, and an active social life. She dates myriad great guys but ends up falling for "Mr. Big," a rich older man who pulls up to her life in a black Lincoln Town Car. Big runs over her heart a few hundred times before leaving her at the altar, all because she didn't answer her cellphone and ease his wedding-day jitters. In the end, both Bridget and Carrie get married, which seems to be their raison d'être. One could argue that these women aren't real and these are just movies, but think about this: Why aren't single men depicted that way? Could you imagine 007 sitting at a diner with his agent friends, crying that the girl he likes hasn't texted him back but had time to post three photos on Facebook? I don't see that happening. The truth is that there aren't any male leads on television or the big screen who spend that much time worrying about whether or not they'll ever find true love. So what does this gross imbalance say about the way society views single women?

The media is always a great reflection of how society treats successful single women. There seem to be only two categories for us: the angry man-hater who is ready to castrate any man who approaches; or the pitiful single Sally. But what about the rest of us? Is it impossible to imagine that a woman can be both single and happy? Why do we call single men "bachelors" and single women "spinsters"? We have come so far in many ways — women can be presidents, army generals, entrepreneurs — but a single woman's relationship status is still treated like a problem that needs to be solved.

Take pop star Taylor Swift, for example. This 10-time Grammy winner has been so scrutinized for penning songs about her ex-boyfriends that as soon as the press gets wind that she is dating someone new, radio DJs start joking about whether the guy will end up on her next album. Meanwhile back at the recording studio Bruno Mars and Ed Sheeran are crooning about their love lives without becoming morning radio fodder. Jennifer Lopez is a great example of how older women are treated. Whether she's dating rap mogul P. Diddy or her backup dancer, fans and critics are quick to put her in a box: she is either a gold digger or a sugar momma.

Her ex-husband Marc Anthony, on the other hand, has been divorced three times and his latest ex-wife, Shannon De Lima, was 20 years his junior, but not once was he described as a sugar daddy or any kind of large predatory feline, so what gives? The rules seem to give women very little room to be their authentic selves. If you date more than five guys, you're a whore; or if you date a younger guy, you're a cougar; and if you embrace your sexuality, well God help us all. Meanwhile Leonardo DiCaprio could start dating a zygote and the worst that would happen is a cute fusion of both their names — Zeonardo.

That being said, have any two single women been under more media scrutiny than actresses Jennifer Aniston and Angelina Jolie? At the time of Aniston's breakup with her then husband Brad Pitt, I was working as an entertainment reporter, and I remember witnessing the way she went from the most envied woman in Hollywood to the most pitied. In case you've been incarcerated for the past 10 to 15 years, let me get you up to speed on the Jennifer Aniston, Brad Pitt, and Angelina Jolie drama. Jennifer was married to Brad. Brad made a movie with Angelina. Brad and Angelina fell in love while making that movie. Then Brad divorced Jennifer and married Angelina. It was quite a scandal at the time and divided women around the world: you were either on TEAM JEN or TEAM ANGELINA. While most people were consumed with the salaciousness of this story, I noticed something far more interesting.

In 2007, two years after Aniston's split from Brad, *Forbes* ranked her as the tenth richest woman in entertainment. Her net worth, $150 million. Not only was her career skyrocketing, but she also had her own perfume line, had signed an eight-figure deal with Aveeno, and was the face of L'Oréal and Smartwater. KA-CHING! At the same time, Aniston was doing charity work for St. Jude Children's Hospital and for Friends of El Faro, which is an organization that improves the lives of orphans in Tijuana, Mexico — but nobody gave a shit. All folks wanted to talk about was poor single Jennifer. If she was photographed standing next to a man, gossip rags and glossy entertainment shows were quick to speculate that this guy might be "The One." Every headline about her found a way to bring up the fact that she was still single, and meanwhile Brad and Angelina had just adopted their seventieth child. In 2015 Jennifer Aniston married actor/director Justin Theroux, ending her 10-year pity party. But wait — I almost forgot — now everyone is on "baby watch." In the summer of 2016 a paparazzi photograph of Aniston on vacation caused a flurry of pregnancy rumours, which prompted a usually closed-mouthed Aniston to rant in the *Huffington Post*, "[Women] are complete with or without a mate, with or without a child. We get to decide for ourselves what is beautiful when it comes to our bodies…. We don't need to be married or mothers to be complete. We get to determine our 'happily ever after' for ourselves.[1] If you're not slow clapping what Jen wrote, well, you might be part of the problem.

As for Angelina, she was depicted in a far more villainous way. This raven-haired, husband-stealing Lolita is best known for wearing a vial of her ex-husband Billy Bob Thornton's blood around her neck and for locking lips with her brother, Jamie, on the Oscar red carpet in 2000. And after Brad left Jen, Angelina was found guilty in the court of public opinion of breaking up the happy Aniston–Pitt home. Her plan was simple: join the cast of *Mr. & Mrs. Smith*. Her part was originally supposed to be played by Nicole Kidman, but due to contract issues Kidman had to drop out of the movie — Jolie probably orchestrated that, too, 'cause you know how devious single women can be. Then all she had to do was convince a perfectly happy Brad to leave his wonderful wife Jennifer, and voila! Mission accomplished. Anyone who believes that's how it all went down is not only naive but also misogynistic. But I'll get to the belief that attractive single women cannot be trusted later on.

Here is the real story. In 2002 Angelina Jolie admitted to veteran journalist Barbara Walters on the magazine show *20/20* that she was a busy working single mom with no time for dating and hadn't had sex in a year. She had just adopted her first child, Maddox, on March 10, 2002, from an orphanage in Cambodia. At age 28, she was already pessimistic about ever being wed again after brief marriages to actors Jonny Lee Miller and Billy Bob Thornton. Jolie was transitioning from the wild child everyone knew into a responsible mother and philanthropist. She had her Billy Bob tattoo removed from her body, and she was beginning to see herself as more than just a box office star. But the world ignored that narrative the minute whispers of an affair with Brad were in the air. Overnight she became every married woman's nightmare, the attractive single woman out to take your husband. And she fit the role perfectly — beautiful, sultry, sexually fluid woman, with a great pair of legs. Poor Brad! He had no chance against her feminine wiles, right? WRONG. The fact is that Brad is an adult, and he made a choice to end his marriage and start a new relationship. People cannot be stolen from other people.

Now Brad Pitt, the one person who should have received all the bad press instead of Jolie, got a pass from all the media outlets when it came to his divorce drama. In September 2016 Brad and Angelina announced the end of their marriage and the world was shocked. Soon after, it was revealed Pitt had drug and alcohol issues, and an altercation on a private plane with his 15-year-old son, Pax, led to an investigation. *GQ* did an interview with a gaunt and sad-looking Pitt, which they described as a "raw conversation."[2] Really, it was was a softball chit-chat about how he was coping with the demise of his marriage. It skimmed over his drug and alcohol issues, instead emphasizing his like-ability and the serenity of this "human father and for-mer husband." *US Weekly*, on the other hand, did what the tabloids always do to women: it cast Angelina as the horrible shrew out for blood, even though she never spoke to journalists or sought sympathy in a teary-eyed photo shoot in the Everglades.

So there you have it — two very successful women reduced to their relationship statuses while the man they both loved played the victim, and no one questions it. If this isn't a single girl problem, I don't know what is.

2

# CHANGING THE NARRATIVE

I DECIDED TO WRITE THIS BOOK IN HOPES of changing the narrative about single women — in particular, those over the age of 30. In spite of all the amazing things women are capable of, society still views single women over 30 as damaged goods, like the unwanted stepchild, the pimple on the ass of dating, the runt of the litter.... You get my point; we get a bad rap. I'm not saying every woman over 30 is a walk in the park, but regardless of our marital status, we aren't any different from anyone else. In my quest to change attitudes, I've also become aware that trying to change people's mindset might be a big waste of time. However, I still feel it needs to be said: SINGLE WOMEN ARE WONDERFUL. Repeat that five times.

SINGLE WOMEN ARE WONDERFUL.
SINGLE WOMEN ARE WONDERFUL.
SINGLE WOMEN ARE WONDERFUL.
SINGLE WOMEN ARE WONDERFUL.
SINGLE WOMEN ARE WONDERFUL.

The challenge is to get society to disassociate single women from words like *crazy, desperate, spinster, sad, lonely, miserable*, and any other negative words. Unfortunately, the blame doesn't solely lie on society. Single women are sometimes their own worst enemies, believing a lot of the nonsense that's said about them and perpetuating their negative man-hating stereotype.

Perhaps it's time to redefine what being single means. Sixty years ago, single women were expected to leave their parents' home only for their matrimonial home, and nearly all forewent a post-secondary education in order to find a good husband. The general thinking around single people over 30 back then was that they were either sick or immoral. *Single* was also a coded word for lesbian, as was the term *confirmed bachelor* for unmarried men suspected of being gay. And suspicion of single people — but especially women — is connected to this institutionalized societal prejudice.

A study conducted by Tobias Greitmeyer in Germany suggested that single people were judged to be less satisfied with their lives, to have lower self-esteem, to be less attractive, to have fewer social skills, and to be more neurotic.[3] There's even a term for this attitude — it's called *singlism*.

We need an update on what it means to be single in the twenty-first century, and it's time to enlighten folks on the reasons for and benefits of this status. Today we are aware that certain levels of maturity, self-awareness, and experience are necessary in order to have healthy relationships. Therefore, singlehood ought to be recognized as a vital time to learn about who you are, what you like, and how to be self-sufficient, and to tackle your insecurities, resolve any trauma you may have suffered in your childhood, tap into your strengths, and learn how to connect and communicate. Instead of chastising women for not being married and encouraging them to go on wild husband-hunting expeditions, society, family, and friends should encourage women to explore who they are before they find a mate to settle down with. This change in attitude could allow all single women to view singlehood as a much-needed sabbatical. This includes the perpetually single, those who fear being alone, the scorned, and the divorced. Single life is time to heal, breathe, re-establish who you are, and tackle any fears you may still have — all without society, friends, and family breathing down your neck.

The number of single people is growing around the world. In the U.K. 4.1 million people live alone, according to the Office of National Statistics. Women are now able to financially support themselves and create full lives for themselves.[4]

Additionally, an increasing number of people don't see being single as a transitional stage, but rather as a permanent state of being. These singles fall into many different categories. There are those who reject the institution of marriage and gender roles; those with demanding careers; and those who have decided that they're not interested in the demands that come with relationships and who don't want to feel guilty about it.

On the other hand, there are some single women who pretend to belong to one of the aforementioned categories but who are really self-sabotaging. Two obvious signs are avoiding any attempt to meet new partners, and having nearly impossible or unrealistic criteria for any potential partner. For any women in that category who are reading this book, I hope it helps you.

For everyone reading, it's time to quit hoping for something magical to change. Happiness will not simply drop into your lap. Try to come to terms with the fact that Prince Charming only exists in fairy tales. Accept that not everyone will love you. You're not perfect, and that's okay. It's more important to love and accept who you are so that no one can affect your self-esteem. Be aware that it's not always about you. Try to stop pointing the finger at others for the bad things that have happened in your life or relationships. Learn that people don't always mean what they say, and they might not always be there for you the way they promised. Stand on your own, and learn how to take care of yourself. Understand that much of the way you see yourself is a result of all the messages you've heard from others. Those words have been ingrained in your head. Forget about everything you've been told about how you should look, how much you should weigh, what you should wear, how you should behave, whom you should marry, or what you owe your family.

I want every single woman who reads this to come to the realization that she deserves to be treated with respect, love, and kindness. I want you never to settle for less. And I want for society to get off our backs! Those are my ultimate goals.

3

# HOW *NOT* TO TALK TO SINGLE PEOPLE

LIKE ANY RELATIONSHIP STATUS, being single comes with a lot of pros and cons, but one of my least favourite parts is the way people talk to us. In my experience the best way to ruin a single woman's mood is to ask her when she's going to get married and have babies. We love that. Some folks won't even let you in the door before hammering you with intrusive questions about your love life. My personal favourites are the unsolicited suggestions about how I should make myself more appealing to potential suitors by being more open and smiling more. There's nothing more aggravating than when a random man walking down the street tells me to smile. Actually, it's enraging. I'm usually caught off guard when it happens, which is frustrating because for the next two or three days I'm consumed with all the things I wish I'd yelled back at him. First of all, I'm not here for his entertainment; second, where did this ridiculous idea that yelling facial expressions at unsuspecting women is a smart thing to do?; and third, who the hell does he think he is? I could go on, but I'll save it for the next asshole who tells me to smile. Sadly, it's not just men who say these ridiculous things. A woman I know confessed that she had been, not once but twice, asked to "smile more" during meetings in her workplace. To look more outwardly pleasant and therefore engaged — because women are expected to look pleasant at all times, right? The first time it happened, she thought, "Well, that's odd," but didn't think too much of it. The second time it happened, a year or two later, she was way more "woke" and was infuriated by the request. She told me, "I wanted to go back and ask if any of my male colleagues had ever been asked to smile more during meetings." For her the worst part was that the request was made by a female superior, at the request of another higher-up female superior. This is never an appropriate request, neither on the street nor in the workplace. At least not until men are regularly asked by strangers and colleagues to look more cheery in public. (The woman decided to give up smiling in meetings and she found herself a new job within the year.)

Years ago I hosted a talk show called *Three Takes*, and we had relationship expert Rabbi Schmuley on the show. During the commercial break he leaned over and said, "You're too pretty to be single." In that moment I found myself at a loss for words — again some man I don't know was giving me his unsolicited comments. I knew in that moment that he wasn't trying to be malicious, but I couldn't help feeling offended. What was he trying to say? Was it supposed to be a compliment or pity? And are relationships only for "pretty" people?

Honestly, I don't think the "single offenders" are even aware of how insulting these types of conversations are, or perhaps I'm giving them too much credit. It might surprise a lot of folks, but a single woman in the twenty-first century has other things going on in her life besides her relationship status. We have drama at our jobs, we might be deciding whether or not to go back to school, or we may have a popular vlog on YouTube or a passion for sports. So why is everyone so interested in making comments to single women about their singleness? How did people get so comfortable with this intrusion?

Personally, I'd like to blame the producers of *The Bachelor*, but this has been going on since before the eighteenth century. Back then it was common practice for families to promise their daughters' hands in marriage in order to secure an alliance between dynasties and guarantee peace between nations. Essentially women were treated like part of the property given in a dowry. A single woman past her prime was viewed as a liability to her family.

A couple of years before I turned 30, I started to notice a change in people's attitudes toward me. All of a sudden, my dating life was at the forefront of every conversation, whether it was with my family, coworkers, or strangers. Men who couldn't have found my G spot with a map and a coal miner's hat were now mentioning my biological clock and making snap judgments about why I wasn't married. When I was 32, I remember this guy asking me how old I was. He then proceeded to tell me what his father had told him: any woman still single over the age of 30 was probably "damaged goods." Once again, I was blindsided by a man's harsh assumption of who I was, and I wondered if all men thought this way. Later, I found out that my inquisitor was single, had been arrested for domestic violence four times, had fathered four children for whom he didn't pay child support, had no credit, and cheated on every women he'd ever been with. But *I* was damaged goods.

I was subjected to these types of conversations so many times that I could fill up an entire book with all the rude, outrageous, and sometimes downright mean things people have said to me about being single. Usually I politely walk away from these spontaneous verbal assaults, but every once in a while I stand my ground and shoot back. Like the time my neighbour told me that she and her husband were discussing why I was still single. They had come to the conclusion that

I must be a lesbian. Oh yeah, if you're a single woman over 35, be aware that at least some of your family and friends think the reason you're still single is because you're a lesbian. I have no idea how they come to this conclusion, but for some reason the heteros think single = gay. That afternoon I was in a fighting mood, so I suggested, "well, why don't you tell your husband to come by my house and see if it's true." She never brought up the topic again.

Unfortunately, there have been occasions when the comments resulted in the termination of a friendship, like the time a girlfriend I'd known since high school — and whom I'd considered one of my best friends — joined the fray. We were in university and she was dating a guy who was verbally, emotionally, and physically abusive to her. Their relationship was full of drama; he gave her STIs, got another girl pregnant, and was always breaking her heart. Other friends told me to stop hanging out with her, but I ignored them because she was my friend and I was loyal — at least until the day she made fun of me for being single. I couldn't believe it. It was one thing for some idiot in a club to be quoting his daddy, but when someone I considered a friend did it, it cut me to the bone. Here she was in a destructive, volatile relationship, but in her mind she was superior to me because I was single. I never spoke to her again after that phone call and never explained why.

As far as I'm concerned, friends should root for each other's happiness whether they're single or not. There is

NOTHING wrong with being single. It's not a disease. Looking at single people with pity is annoying to them. Almost as annoying as setting them up with your husband's friend who has zero social skills and residual issues with his ex who left him in a one-bedroom basement apartment. Oh, and spare us the story about your best friend's cousin's sister, who met a guy online and married him six months later. We are not perishable items on a grocery store shelf.

At times I've played around with the idea of turning the tables on these obnoxious single-lady haters and asking them about their nonexistent sex lives, or if they are as bored in their relationships as they look. And how many tries did it take to figure out their partner's Ashley Madison account password? But that would be unladylike, not to mention a major downer at the dinner party, and I love a good dinner party.

In order for the conversations to start changing, we single women have to stand up for ourselves and stop playing into the stereotype that we're all desperately seeking marriage and children. The next time the words "don't worry it will happen" (or any other tasteless cliché), come out of someone's mouth, tell them how the comment makes you feel. Then tell that person about what's going on in your life, or talk about a news story you read, or ask them a question about their life, or just walk away without saying a word. Whatever you choose to do, just keep in mind that it's not your job to explain or defend why you're single.

# 4

## EVEN DISNEY GETS IT

GROWING UP I WAS VERY GIRLY, from the silk ribbons in my hair right down to my frilly socks. And, like most little girls, I loved watching Disney movies and I especially loved the Disney princesses. Snow White, Cinderella, Belle, Ariel, Rapunzel, Aurora — I was infatuated with all of them. Watching a beautiful girl get rescued by a prince on a noble steed was magical to me and also very normal. And why wouldn't it be? That was all I'd ever seen.

As a child I also knew that this was make-believe. I knew mice couldn't turn into horses, mermaids weren't real, and guys didn't travel by steed, at least not in the city I grew up in. It wasn't until I went to a friend's princess-themed wedding — complete with puffy white dress, tiara, and horse and carriage — that I came to the realization that not all of us viewed Disney movies as make-believe. For some women this concept of being rescued by a man was a real-life goal.

Most of the classic Disney damsel-in-distress plot lines were written in the 1950s, a time when a woman's main ambition was to get married and have children. Life has changed a lot since then, and so has Disney. Their leading ladies are no longer waiting to be awakened by a kiss from the one true love; now they're kicking ass and saving the world.

Child psychologist Dr. Jennifer L. Hartstein, author of *Princess Recovery*, summarizes that Disney characters like Cinderella promote the idea that if a girl is pretty enough and has fancy enough clothes and shoes, she'll find love and be popular. Alternatively, Hardstein believes children should be taught the value of intelligence, generosity, and passion.[5]

The Disney movie *Frozen* flipped the script on the traditional princess storyline by having the bond between two sisters take centre stage. *Maleficent* and *Inside Out* also stepped away from the typical formula of "boy rescues girl" and showed young women as strong, complex beings who didn't need to be saved. Disney's newest leading lady is Moana. Her goal is to save the world. Funnily enough, Disney has decided to embrace the idea that a woman can be okay without a man proposing on bended knee. This very idea is the primary reason I wrote this book. Now, if Disney, which has been making these types of movies for over six decades, can find a way to shift its narrative, then surely society can stop talking to single women as though they are sad, lonely creatures who need a man to complete their lives, right?

If everyone can agree not to tell little girls that life is a fairy tale, and that they shouldn't expect a handsome man with a chiselled jawline to swoop in to save the day, then why is there such resistance from mothers, grandmothers, cousins, and fathers? When are the people closest to us going to stop berating the young women in their family for not being married with a couple of kids?

This is not an anti-marriage sentiment as much as it is a "hey, let's stop treating women like it's 1942" idea. Instead of chastising a woman for being single, we should refocus our attention on celebrating all the things she's got going on in her life. A Disney princess no longer needs a prince to experience true love, and I say if it's good enough for Elsa, it's good enough for the rest of us.

# 5

# WHY ARE YOU STILL SINGLE?

*"Dating after thirty is easy.*
*It's like riding a bike,*
*But the bike is on fire,*
*And the ground is on fire.*
*Everything is on fire*
*Because you are in hell."*
— Unknown

"WHY ARE YOU STILL SINGLE?" Personally, I hate this question. I'm going to assume that if you're reading this book, you've been asked this question a million times, and you hate it too. First of all, there's so much judgment in the question itself. The person may as well ask "What's wrong with you? Why doesn't anyone want to love you? How come no one wants to stick around?" At least, that's what "Why are you still single?" sounds like in my head. I've always been curious about what kind of answer someone who asks this rude question is looking for. But again, I'm acutely aware that it seems socially acceptable to corner a single woman and needle her about her single status. Perhaps those who ask this question think we're all living like the Unabomber, off in some secluded shed in the woods, or torturing some poor soul the way Cathy Bates's character does in *Misery*.

I've also noticed that way more women than men ask why I'm still single. I have no idea why. Perhaps I talk about relationships more with women than I do with men, or maybe men feel more comfortable talking about a single woman behind her back than to her face. In my personal experience, if a man is asking, he's either interested in me or he wants to find out if I'm a desperate girl looking for an engagement ring and a baby. Women, on the other hand, are way more malicious, and — let me be specific — I'm talking about married women. There's an arrogance that many married women have when talking to their single girlfriends who are over 30. I'm obviously not referring to all married women, of course. Particularly those who found their partners later in life or who have been divorced are more understanding of their single sisters, but the rest of them — well, let's just say they're a tough crowd.

I'll never forget the meeting I had with a 50-something-year-old radio executive. Before I could even sit down in her office, she asked me, "Are you still single? What's the problem?" I smiled politely and shrugged my shoulders. But how dare she? From that moment on I lost all respect for her. That was supposed to have been a pitch meeting, not a personal-life chit-chat. Not only was her question out of line, but her tone made it clear that she saw my lack of spouse as a shortcoming and a clear indication that there must be something wrong with me. Afterwards I couldn't help but wonder if I were a man, would she have asked me the same question in the same way? I can't possibly know the answer. In any case, I held my tongue and went off to do what had I originally planned: work hard and be successful.

Sometimes the inquiry comes off as a backhanded compliment. It's kind of like saying, "You're pretty and you seem nice, so what's the problem? Why haven't you been snatched up yet?" Most of us are already asking ourselves the same questions. Regardless of the asker's intention, it's the one question single people get asked the most, and it's also an impossible question to answer. I mean, what am I supposed to say? "Nobody effin' likes me." Or maybe "Didn't you hear, I'm cuckoo for Cocoa Puffs!" At times it also feels like a married woman's way of being passive-aggressive: "I'm better than you are because a man put a ring on my finger."

The worst part is I think a lot of single women believe that propaganda. The real truth is that not all married folks are happy; some of them are absolutely miserable, sleeping in separate bedrooms, and trying to make the best of their bad situations. From the outside it can be deceiving, especially if you want what your married friends have. But you can't judge a relationship you are not in.

There are a lot of great things about being single, but that question, "Why are you single?", can really put you on the spot, especially if you don't want to be single. Most of the single ladies I've met are trying their best to meet a great guy, whether online or on blind dates, and it's not easy. I compare dating to sifting through a bin at a second-hand clothing store. You've gotta go through a lot of crap other people threw away before you find what you like, and even then you have to smell it, check it for stains, look at the stitching, and see if it even fits before you bring it home.

During my research, I found a lot of sobering facts about single life that may help you understand why you're single. First, 44 percent of the population in North America is single.[6] That means nearly half of the people you encounter at the mall, in your office building, or on a busy street are single, so you're not alone. The ratio of single women to men is 100 to 86, so we outnumber the guys by quite a bit. And 40 million people use online dating sites, but the number of engagement rings sold has dipped over the past 10 years.[7] As a side note, the rates of reported cases of chlamydia, gonorrhea, and infectious syphilis among men 25 to 29 years old have been rising since the early 2000s. Just thought you'd like to know that little tidbit.

Aside from the fact that fewer people are getting married in the twenty-first century (according to *Time* magazine, 25 percent of Millennials will never get married),[8] there are a lot of single ladies who are standing in their own way of getting married. I'm not a big fan of blaming others for the way things are, but it seems there are generations of grown women out there with the notion that one day actor Idris Elba (who, by the way, says he'll never get married again) might come along and sweep them off their feet. In truth, there is no glass slipper, no magical kiss, and definitely no storybook "happily ever after" ending. This unrealistic ideology is a recipe for disaster. In the real world, successful relationships need essentials like communication, compromise, honesty, respect, support, love, and a lot of hard work. If you're waiting for your perfect partner to swoop in and rescue you from your life, you may be waiting forever.

In order to be a truly successful partner, you have to be a successful single. That means you're not waiting for the "perfect man" to come along and resolve unpaid debts, emotional baggage, or any other area of your life where you are unhappy. First you need to take a long, hard look at your life and ask yourself what you're waiting for your perfect partner to fix or provide. Then make a plan to get it done on your own. I know it's easy to get

## Dating Horror Story #1
### Christine H.

I remember once I had a very good-looking guy with a solid profile contact me. On his profile it noted he was looking for long-term dating and a relationship. We began by exchanging a few messages and then proceeded to move our chat over to Yahoo Messenger.

Of course, being the cautious "single girl", I made a special account purely for online dating that would not disclose any of my personal information. That is, not until I felt comfortable.

However, it appears that some males don't have the same need for security. On a whim I googled the guy's username and email. What followed was a string of hits on a site for casual sex. When I clicked one of the hits, I found myself looking at a full frontal of the guy with a very happy penis … smiling at me! Accompanying this were multiple angles of said guy with "duck face" … the same guy I had been chatting with!

On our next chat I worked into the conversation a question about sex sites and the like. He said he was completely opposed to them. I said "Really?!" Then I attached the link to his body pic. "That's funny because your body tells a different story!"

distracted by stories about video vixens and Instagram models marrying financially successful men and start wishing you could have that kind of luck, but as my mother always says, "Every form of refuge has its price." If someone is paying your way and in control of your happiness, then they have the power to take it all away. A lot of us are paying too much attention to superficial things like his facial hair, his action figure collection, or the fact that he doesn't like Japanese food. (I actually have a girlfriend who stopped dating a guy because he didn't like sushi.) Remember that the men you date are human, with their own strengths and weaknesses, and they shouldn't be treated like an ATM. You are not perfect, and expecting perfection from someone else is ridiculous.

If you want, you can have a laundry list of superficial attributes you'd like your future partner to have, but online dating will break your spirit — well, it broke mine anyway. In 2008, Internet dating took flight, and speed dating, text-message breakups, and Tinder hook-ups followed shortly thereafter. Dismissing one partner for another has become the norm. While I'm a huge fan of having lots of options, let's face it: it has become more difficult to connect with someone. I've often felt as though I have to prove to a man that I'm worth a phone call or a date while, at the same time, dodging strong sexual advances before we even learn each other's last names. And while you're swiping right and updating your profile picture, your prince may come along and get lost in the crowd. Instead of riding high off of all the attention, do yourself a favour and slow down, pay attention, and give yourself permission to date less-than-perfect men. But let me make myself clear: I am not encouraging women to date men they don't want to go out with or to accept dates with anyone who asks. Just ensure you're not getting in your own way by letting a good one go because he didn't check every single item on your laundry list of requirements.

There should be negotiable and non-negotiable items. For example, needing a man to be six foot four should be negotiable unless you're a six-foot glamazon yourself — and even then, ask yourself how important that is. A long time ago someone told me I shouldn't ask him to be something I'm not. Today's fast-paced online dating culture definitely makes it easier to meet a lot more dating prospects, but at the same time it's increasingly difficult to get to know a person before moving on to the next tempting option. Now, I can already hear you yelling at me, "Andrea it's not women with the short attention spans — it's the men!" I hear you, and I'm just as frustrated with their behaviour as you are. DeVon Franklin, co-author of *The Wait*, put it best when he posted on Instagram, "We date self-ishly, unconcerned about the collateral damage we do to women just so we can find happiness in the moment." This so wonderfully summed up how dating in the twenty-first century feels for a lot of us single ladies. We can't control any man's behaviour, but we can make sure that we don't end up as receptacles for their garbage. So again, never settle for anyone who doesn't treat you with kindness and compassion, or for someone who is unwilling to invest time in you.

In the majority of relationship books I've read, writers dismiss the idea of there being one single person on the entire planet who is right for you. Again this notion of "The One" was probably born out of the fairy tale in which only one girl fits that glass slipper. The idea that you may have missed your opportunity to marry "The One" is rubbish, so don't despair. In fact, all of those bad dates and broken hearts are proof that there are lots of "ones" out there, like the first one, the smart one, the rich-but-emotionally-unavailable one, the great-in-bed-but-not-so-smart one. The only thing you need to do is stay open-minded, be your best self, and learn valuable lessons from each person you date. That way, when "Good Ones" come along, you can spot them, date them, and decide who's the one for you.

# 6

# IS DATING DEAD?

WE ARE LIVING IN A TIME WHEN tons of experts are doling out advice about how to date, and there are many articles on the subject: how to improve your online dating profile, where to meet the perfect guy, where to go on your first date, the best cities to find a date, how to date after divorce, and my personal favourite, how to date on a budget. It's funny to think that 100 years ago this kind of advice would have been either scoffed at or completely ignored; the expectations then were that you would meet and marry someone from your village. It was also taboo for a woman (other than a prostitute!) to have multiple sexual partners, and divorce was rarely an option. Things have changed completely, for better or worse — and I say that because all of the freedom and options we have today don't seem to benefit a lot of single people. Actually, the opposite appears to be true.

While I was working as a lifestyle expert on *Steven and Chris*, a nationally syndicated lifestyle talk show, the number one thing I discovered was that a lot of people are confused by modern dating, except of course the Millennials. My 16-year-old cousin, Eric, told me he only dates girls he meets online. I asked him about the girls in his school, and he promptly told me that they were okay, but he had more options online. Plus it was easier to talk to a girl on his cellphone than it was to approach a girl at school. This sounded crazy to me because I grew up at a time when we only dated people from our school or neighbourhood. A boy had to muster the courage to ask a girl out face to face, and in order to speak to her he had to call her house and probably speak to one of her parents first. Now sites like Instagram, Facebook, and Snapchat eliminate that process altogether.

Today everyone from teenagers to senior citizens are hooking up with other singles via their smartphones. It's no longer necessary to sit through a bad date — your online dating profile can provide you with other available options while you finish your drinks with the dud sitting across from you. These are the times we are living in, folks, and if you've been off the market for a while it can be very intimidating to get back on the dating highway, when it feels like everyone else has a brick on the accelerator.

Personally, I feel that modern dating is a bit of a shit-storm, and online dating has adversely affected every-one's attention spans. I know "commitment phobia" existed before, but now it seems most singles have dating ADHD, and the bad news is there's no dating equivalent of Ritalin or Adderall to slow everyone down. Random hook-ups are not new — we've all heard about the key parties and free-spirited sex in the 1960s — but online dating sites have caused a new type of sexual revo-lution. Now with just one swipe to the right you can find a sexual partner who's only a few blocks away, free of charge. Finding true love and getting married have become a competitive reality show, where roughly nine million viewers gather

**CUFFING SEASON**

The period of time during the fall/winter months when you cuff yourself to someone so you can stay in rather than having to be on the prowl in the cold. People usually "uncuff" themselves once the snow starts to melt and spring rolls around.

every Monday night to watch a man or woman hand out long-stemmed roses to twenty-five well-groomed prospects. The finale is like watching the dating Super Bowl. Fans cheer for their favourite as the final two con-testants battle it out, faces streaming with tears as we all wait to see who gets the ring. Marriage is supposed to be the ultimate goal, but few, if any, make it to the happily-ever-after stage once the cameras are turned off.

## Dating Horror Story #2
### Reeshma K.

I once went out on a marathon date with a guy. He asked all the right questions, paid for our coffees and snacks, and asked me to continue the conversation since it was going so well. He seemed really interested and asked me questions about my job, picking my brain about the clinical work I do, and showing a genuine interest in my interests. We continued the date over dinner, and then I dropped him back at his place (I had my car with me) because it was getting late.

He invited me in for a tea then proceeded to pull out his guitar and serenade me with a song! It had been a ten-hour date!!! Our night ended with a prolonged hug, a peck on the cheek, and a promise to call.

That call never came, and I never heard from him again.

Once the victor has been chosen, viewers are quick to forget the most recent love affair and eager for a new favourite to cheer on.

Personally I'm not a fan of these types of programs. If anything, I find the whole premise of trying to find true love on camera to be a complete farce. It makes a mockery of the institution of marriage and turns beautiful, educated women into delusional, sobbing, catty little girls. The voyeurs of these cotton-candy televised love affairs are predominantly women. But in my research for this book I also found it has become a lot more common for men to date multiple women at the same time. Dating sites like eHarmony, Match.com, and Tinder have made it easier to do so, and — surprise, surprise — women don't like this new trend. What's confusing to me is the way conservative women will give a blogger like Natalie Brooke a hard time about her views on why society only celebrates women when they get married but they're totally okay with a competitive reality show that pits 25 women against each other for the love of one guy. What message are we sending single women?

MONKEY BAR

The way people swing from relationship to relationship.

TEXTLATIONSHIP

A relationship that exists solely via texting. Someone is texting you all the time, but you don't hang out in person.

"Ghosting" is a new trend in the dating world. The term refers to a style of ending a relationship. You're dating someone and for no apparent reason they just disappear without any warning or explanation. Phone calls, text messages, and Facebook posts are met with dead silence. It's the new cowardly way to end relationships. While the term may be new, the concept isn't. I have an aunt who was ghosted at her wedding back in the 1970s.

Ghosting robs the other person of closure. By law, an employer must provide a reason for firing an employee, but in today's dating world such notice is a luxury. Could this be a side effect of the monkey bar? I've spoken to many singles who say it's too awkward to tell a person the truth about why they've lost interest because they don't want to directly hurt their feelings. Instead they would prefer the person takes the hint and stops calling. Stop and think for a minute: if we all stop treating each other with respect this way, what will the dating world be like in 10 or 20 years?

## HAUNTING

When someone who previously ghosted you comes back "from the dead" by friending you on Facebook, following you on Instagram, or suddenly "liking" your posts.

## FBO

Facebook Official: declaring your relationship status on your social media profile.

Late-night texting, or the "booty call," became a part of the playbook back in 1997 when the movie by the same name, starring comedians Jamie Foxx and Tommy Davidson, became a box-office hit. Since then people have used the term as a warning to women about men who are only contacting them for sex. Today it's called "Netflix and chill." The terms mean more or less the same thing, but admittedly the latter sounds way more innocent. According to Wikipedia, this English slang phrase uses the invitation to watch Netflix together as a euphemism for sex. The term gained popularity in 2009 on social media sites Twitter, Facebook, and Vine. Its regular use by Millennials on social media went from being an Internet meme into general use.

BENCHING

When you keep someone at arm's reach (someone who is probably interested in you) while you pursue another relationship. You keep that person "on the bench" in case the relationship you're pursuing doesn't pan out.

On the subject of casual hook-ups, they seem to be everywhere. Hollywood is even making romantic comedies about it. *Friends with Benefits* is a movie about two successful young people who are jaded by their past relationships and decide instead to have a purely sexual relationship. Spoiler alert: they end up falling for each other. Casual hook-ups are woven into the lyrics of many pop songs played on mainstream radio, and a whole generation of young adults have been raised in a unique time when casual hook-ups have a strong presence in their popular culture. It almost begs the question: is dating dead?

In the past 10 years many studies have been done on the subject of hook-up culture because of its new-found popularity. The General Social Survey, a national data set of households in the United States, found that young people between the ages of 18 and 25 are having more casual sex and way less romantic sex than previous generations. As for the death of dating, the same study found that the vast majority (78 percent) has had sex with a romantic partner, but the number of people who have had sex with a friend or casual date has gone up 10–15 percent over the past few years, which means there are more "friends with benefits" encounters occurring than sex with random strangers.[9]

# 7

# MY LOVE/HATE
# RELATIONSHIP
# WITH ONLINE DATING

DOES ONLINE DATING WORK? Fuck if I know. Personally, I'm not a fan. Never have been, and never will be. I've always been suspicious of getting things off the Internet. Everything always looks great in the pictures, but when it arrives, it rarely ever meets your expectations. For the purposes of this book I joined five online dating sites for three weeks to see if I was wrong. I encountered a lot of shallow exchanges, like "Nice smile," and a few very direct messages. One guy, who had a convertible Porsche as his profile picture, wanted to know my favourite sexual position. That was his conversation starter. I guess homeboy wasn't into beating around the bush — he obviously preferred spreading its legs and diving into it.

## Dating Horror Story #3
### Alma D.

While working on a campaign in Kansas City, MO, I was out at a bar with a group of friends one night and noticed a guy with shoulder-length turquoise-coloured hair who was also noticing me. He looked like he could have been a member of Poison or some such 80s hair band; he was wearing a little makeup and punk clothes.

I don't remember how we started talking by the pinball machine, but eventually we left the bar together and walked to his hotel, where he was staying with his bandmates (they were an L.A.-based band on tour). They were staying in a suite with a living room and bedroom, and he took me to the bedroom where his friend was watching TV on the other bed. We were sitting on his bed smoking when he pulled out a pocketknife. As he peeled out the large blade, he asked if I'd ever been cut before. He said it like an invitation rather than a threat, as if it was something that was supposed to turn me on, but of course it scared the hell out of me.

I didn't want to run in case that provoked some kind of predator/prey game that could end badly, so I tried to maintain control. I told him we should go into the living room so we could have more privacy, and he followed me; this got me closer to the exit. When he suggested we have sex, I told him I was very promiscuous (this was a lie) and hadn't been tested for STDs in a long time, so I wasn't sure if I had anything, and of course I didn't want to get him sick. With this, I was able to leave unharmed and without him chasing me.

At one point I became obsessed with swiping left and right on the photos of men living within a five-kilometre radius of my house. Seeing the kind of profile pictures men used to attract the opposite sex was also fascinating. There's the selfie-in-the-bathroom guy, the look-at-my-expensive car guy, the sunglasses guy, the group-photo guy, the posed-with-my-pet guy, the vacation-photo guy. Hands-down, my favourite was the guy who posted a picture of a woman giving birth in a delivery room. I mean, come on, ladies, who wouldn't want to date that prince? That said, I have heard countless stories about Tinder couples and Match.com couples tying the knot. Maybe it was my attitude about online dating that affected the outcome. Even though I went in with an open heart, to be completely honest, I have always had a strong feeling that the right guy for me isn't on eHarmony or Plenty of Fish. Actually, I don't see him having a huge social media presence at all, though I can't explain why I feel this way. But I do have a funny online dating story I want to share with you.

A couple of years ago I was invited to a swanky dinner party that boasted a guest list of rock stars, authors, and politicians. The moment I walked into the private room where we were gathered, a gorgeous six-foot-tall man caught my attention. He was clean-shaven, with short brown hair and green eyes. Slowly but surely I made my way over to where he was and introduced myself. He looked even better up close. After I wooed him with my dazzling ability to make small talk, he said to me, "Where are you sitting? Let's sit together." Winner! *Gagnant!* Before long we were talking as if we'd known each other for years. He disclosed that he had to get permission from a judge and his parole officer to come to the party because he had just finished a four-year jail sentence for theft and was currently living in a halfway house. Needless to say, I was taken aback — not only by the information he had just plopped on the table, but also by the nonchalant manner in which he delivered it. Instead of making up an excuse and fleeing the scene, I decided to ask him what it had been like in prison. What had he stolen? And whether he was excited about dating or, more specifically, having sex.

The answers to the first two questions were not half as interesting as the answer he gave me to the last question. "I've gotten plenty of ass thanks to online dating," he responded, a mischievous smile on his face, "How?" I inquired. According to this handsome former inmate, he and the other men at the halfway house were given cellphones to help them find jobs, but they also used them to go online and swipe right on as many women as they could. They'd talk to the ladies they matched with, make plans to meet for a coffee or a drink, and if things went well, the rendezvous would end up at her place and they'd have sex. "It's that easy?" I asked, "Yeah," he responded while slathering butter on a dinner roll. "What do you tell the women when they ask about your job or where you live?" I asked. "It generally doesn't come up, but if she asks I tell her the truth." My eyes widened. "What about paying the bill? You're not working, so how do you figure that part out?" And this is the part that really got me. He said, "Honestly, I've had sex with a bunch of women, and I've never been asked about paying. Actually, I wish sometimes they'd make it more of a challenge for me."

# *Online Dating:*

## AN INTERVIEW WITH JULIE SPIRA

In order to help you navigate the online dating jungle, I wanted to interview a person who really knows what's going on. Online dating expert and dating coach Julie Spira is the bestselling author of *The Perils of Cyber-Dating: Confessions of a Hopeful Romantic Looking for Love Online.* Here is a transcript from our conversation:

**Andrea Bain:** What are three of the most important things online daters should know?

**Julie Spira:** Online dating is a numbers game. You need to play to win. While it can be overwhelming at first, or you might get frustrated not finding compatible matches, know that it's a big digital playground, and it only takes one.

**AB:** What is the best way to avoid men who are online but only looking for a quick sexual encounter?

**JS:** There are a lot of men looking for hook-ups.

Guess what? There are a lot of women interested in casual sex as well. While you can't avoid being contacted by someone who's interested in a casual encounter or hook up, you can be proactive in your profiles. For instance, when I work with my dating coaching clients, I always say, "Looking to hook up? Swipe left." That sends a message to someone who isn't interested in a serious relationship to move on to the next pretty face.

**AB:** What is the best way to get the conversation from online to face to face?

**JS:** Looking for love online is just the method to meet someone offline or IRL (in real life). Having online chemistry doesn't always transfer to offline chemistry. My recommendation is to start chatting or emailing someone you find interesting, and yes, ladies, you can email the man first! After a few email or text exchanges, let the guy know you'd like to talk on the phone, and ask for his digits and a good time to call. Schedule a phone date, but keep it short. I recommend no more than 20 minutes. Set a timer if you have to because if your phone date is going well and you can talk for hours on end, you should end

the call so you can continue the conversation face to face on a date. After 20 minutes, your goal is to put a date on the calendar. If you're not feeling it, then thank him for his time and wish him well.

Make sure you meet in a public place, and always let a friend know whom you're having the date with and where you're going. Excuse yourself when it's time to put on more lipstick, and check in with your buddy from the restroom to let them know how your date is going.

**AB:** There are lots of creeps online. Should you do a background check before agreeing to meet with someone?

**JS:** These days everyone is doing a background check at some point, but before you meet the person, let Google and social media play digital detective. Google his email address and phone number, take his profile photo and post it to Google Images to see what pops up, and hop over to Facebook to see if you have any real friends in common. If so, ask a mutual friend for a recommendation. If the date goes well, snap a photo of the two of you and text it to your friend to keep it light and fun.

**AB:** What's the best strategy for grabbing the attention of a guy you like online?

**JS:** The best way to grab someone's attention is to reach out and say hello. If you're attracted to his profile, then compliment him on his gorgeous blue eyes or the photo of him hiking in the mountains. The more specific you are about what his passions are, the more he'll see that you're the real deal.

**AB:** How accurate are the personality tests on online dating sites?

**JS:** I happen to love dating algorithms and am intrigued by the matching, but then again, someone can be a 99 percent match with someone they have zero chemistry with. At the end of the digital day, having a high match percentage is a great icebreaker to reach out to someone. For example, I would say, "Hi … The computer thinks we're a 94 percent match, so I thought I'd say hello. Do you think the computer knows best?" Keep it light and flirty and read how someone answers their questions on dating sites. As a starter, that can really tell a lot about compatibility.

**AB:** Is it worth it to sign up for the online dating sites that charge a fee?

**JS:** Yes. Although there are many free sites out there, many dating sites and mobile dating apps also have premium features that allow you to browse anonymously so you don't appear to be a stalker if you look at someone's profile 10 times a day, or that can help you rank higher and be more visible. For the price of a daily coffee, there's no reason not to sign up for a paid site and a free site to see which you prefer. Chances are that most singles are members of at least three dating sites and apps these days, so you might view the same person on multiple sites. If that happens, I suggest you keep it to yourself. Both of you know you're on multiple dating sites, so don't say, "Hey, I saw you on Tinder and Bumble!" It's a buzzkill, and you just might be taken off his or her date card altogether.

# 8

# CHASING YOUR OWN TAIL

SO, YOU LIKE THIS GUY. Maybe you *really* like him. He checks all the boxes on your long list of things you want in your Mr. Perfect. You pre-write cute, sexy text messages to send him or post provocative profile pictures hoping he'll double tap. Every time he posts something on his social media you like it and leave a comment. Most of your correspondence is initiated by you. He responds to your messages — sometimes right away, but other times it might take him two, three, maybe even five days to get back to you. When he does get back to you, you and your bestie turn into forensic scientists analyzing each word trying to decipher any hidden meaning behind his "check you later" sign-off.

Thanks to social media you can keep track of your crush's every move, see who his friends are, and of course look for any signs of a girlfriend. I'm not going to bring up the fact that you're probably stalking his ex-girlfriend's Instagram and Facebook pages, just know that I know. I know this because I've been there, done that, and got the restraining order. I'm joking about the restraining order, of course — I'm too slick to get caught! As you probably already know, you're not alone in this strange dating behaviour. In the twenty-first century there's a very familiar storyline that goes a little something like this: "Hey, you're cute. Let's be friends with benefits because I don't want a relationship. But I *would* like you to treat me like I'm your boyfriend. That includes your loyalty, sex, and special attention, but don't ever forget that I can do whatever I want. If you break this agreement and get upset at anytime, I will quickly remind you that we're not together because I told you from the start that I don't want a relationship."

## BREADCRUMBING

When someone gives you juuuuust enough that you think you may have a chance at a relationship. They never actually follow through, leading you on like Hansel and Gretel following their trail of breadcrumbs.

If you've never been strung along, well, congratulations. You are smarter than a lot of women. But for the rest of us, myself included, this has become the norm. It's a part of the dating process, a shitty part, but one where

## Dating Horror Story #4
### Stacey T.

I went on a first date with Bob* after we met through friends. It was Halloween day and he thought it would be fun to go to Screemers at the CNE. A haunted house on Halloween? Amazing! He asked me to meet him at the McDonald's close to the CNE so we could take advantage of the free coffee promotion that was happening that day. Sign #1?

We walked over to the haunted house, sharing some light conversation on the way. He told me that the previous year he and two of his friends actually went trick-or-treating. They were 23 at the time. Sign #2?

We finally got to the haunted house and walked through the attraction. It was actually pretty scary! I grabbed his arm a few times (which I'm sure was also part of his plan!) as all kinds of people, objects, and screams emerged from places and spaces. The last room contained a reenactment of the *Texas Chainsaw Massacre*. I saw a body on a table and just knew that it was going to pop up and scare the bejesus out of us. Was I ever wrong! As we focused all of our attention on the body, a man with a huge chainsaw popped out of a closet! I let out a scream and jumped toward Bob, who, in his own fear, decided that the best approach would be to grab me by the back of my shirt and throw me toward the man with the chainsaw. Then he ran out of the room at top speed, leaving me behind crouching in a corner as the chainsaw came closer and closer to my face.

Ever gotten a sympathetic look from a man with a chainsaw? Yeah. First and last date. Thanks for the free coffee, Bob.

*Name has been changed.

you quickly learn that the first rule in relationships is never to be someone's number two — pun intended — because it's a shitty place to be.

These types of relationships start off pretty innocently. Maybe you meet him at a party or through friends. There's an immediate physical attraction, but it's too early to say what you two will become. The more you see him, the more you like him, and soon he's all you can think about. The only problem is, well, there are a few problems, but the main problem is that you like him way more than he likes you, but you haven't figured that out yet. You're so hungry for his attention that every time he tosses you a bread crumb of attention, you feed off it, convincing yourself that's enough to keep the flame burning for your love. As I mentioned before, this type of guy usually lets you know right off the bat that he's not that into you by saying things like "I'm really busy"; "I just got out of a relationship"; "I like you but I'm not looking for anything serious right now." Or he doesn't say anything at all. His total avoidance of the whole relationship topic is another clear indication of how he feels about you. At the same time he'll do things that are confusing. He might give you a cute nickname, or every once in a while he'll do something really sweet. It feels as if something's there, but deep down you know something is a little off.

**PHUBBING**

Snubbing your partner to pay attention to your phone.

In my mid-20s I began chasing my own tail for a guy that I'd had a crush on since I was in high school. We had grown up in the same neighbourhood, so I would run into him from time to time, but back then talking to him seemed like a pipe dream. At the time, my dating life was a lot of "I want him, he wants someone else, and someone different wants me." As a result I was determined to get the guy I wanted to want me back. At first it was all going according to plan. I got all of his attention and I loved it. We hung out at his house a lot (clue #1). He'd return my phone calls or texts, but not right away; sometimes it would take an hour or two days (clue #2). He introduced me to his mother once, and I was sure that it meant something, but he also avoided meeting mine at all cost (clue #3). Soon people were noticing our little "are they or aren't they" dance, and by "people" I mean friends and strangers alike. The energy between us made it obvious that something was going on, but at the same time I couldn't call him my boyfriend.

This went on for nearly a year and a half until one of his close friends pulled me aside and said, "Listen, I like you and you're a really nice girl, but get a clue. It's never going to happen, and sometimes you have to know when to move one." To say my heart was broken would be an understatement. I was so angry with him for making me look stupid to everyone, but after I calmed down, I realized I was just angry with myself. How could I have let this bullshit go on for so long? Why didn't I initiate a conversation about our relationship? Why was I so happy to get a fraction of this man's attention? Really, I hadn't wanted the dream to be over. Deep down I knew that if I had asked him for any kind of commitment, he would've most definitely said no. I paid more attention to his words than to his actions, and I knew he liked me but not the way I deserved or wanted to be liked back. Sadly, it took his best friend taking pity on me for me to face the truth.

What I learned from that situation was invaluable. First off, texting isn't courting. If you think you are in a relationship with a man, but 90 percent of your communicating is done via text message, you are NOT in a relationship. A man who likes you will pick up the phone and call to make plans to see you. This new era of technology in dating has confused a lot of us into thinking that getting a "wyd" or "u up" message or an eggplant emoji actually means something. Don't be afraid to ask him what kind of relationship he wants from you because his answer could save you a lot of time and energy. There's also another way to find out if what you're feeling is real or all in your head: stop texting, emailing, calling, and stalking his social media for a week. I want you to ghost him for seven whole days. This may seem extreme, but if he really likes you he will notice that your attentions have stopped.

Now if he doesn't notice your absence and you still want to continue the situation, maybe you should ask yourself why you don't think you deserve more than a text back two days later. Maybe it's a timing thing, and maybe he's just not ready yet. Maybe you're hoping to have a Hollywood ending like Carrie and Big. But no matter the reason(s), it's an unhealthy practice to exaggerate your place in a man's heart.

Constantly being disappointed by a man you like shouldn't be the final chapter of your love life, but whether or not your next relationship is going to be a blessing or another lesson is completely up to you. The ball is in your court.

# 9

# *SETTLING* IS SUCH AN UGLY WORD

I HAVE A CONFESSION TO MAKE. At one point I seriously considered settling down with a guy I sorta liked just to stop everyone from busting my lady balls about not being married. I was so desperate for people to talk to me about anything but my relationship status that I actually contemplated this drastic move. I wanted so badly for my married friends to invite me to all of the secret couples gatherings I was left out of without explanation. I wanted to joke about putting on a few extra pounds and letting the hair on my lady parts grow because my husband had already legally tethered himself to me — even though I would never do that. I could use being married as an excuse to not show up for events: "Sorry, we can't make it. Tom has a work thing." My ex-boyfriends would stop sending me DMs. And my mother, my poor, long-suffering mother, could finally face the ladies in her church. I was also sick and tired of seeing pity in people's eyes when I told them, "No, I'm still single." But I couldn't bring myself to do something so selfish. I mean, can you imagine your spouse being asked why they chose you and having their response be, "Well, I was holding out for someone special, but I got tired of waiting. Then Andrea came along and I said to myself, 'She'll do.'" I. Would. Die.

The only settling anyone should be doing is settling out of court or settling the dinner cheque. Never when it comes to relationships. The pressure to settle gets to a lot of single women, and it's easy to see why. Take a 34-year-old woman, add two pushy parents who want grandchildren, send her five to ten wedding invitations a year, sprinkle on a few bad Tinder dates, add a run in with her ex-boyfriend (the one she dated for five years, who went on to propose to his next girlfriend after six months of dating), and have everyone she talks to ask her why she's still single. Top it off with her OB/GYN warning her about her declining fertility, and there you have it, folks: a woman primed and ready to settle.

**SWERVING**

Dodging someone who is romantically interested in you but whom you don't like in the same way.

There's actually a name for this desperate feeling. It's called Single Inferiority Complex or SIC for short. Especially if you've ever been attacked, pitied, harassed, or accused of being too picky, you might suffer from SIC. I, myself, have suffered from SIC for years. All those times I was blindsided by mean-spirited questions and awful theories as to why no one has walked me down the aisle. For a long time I avoided certain social events like anniversary parties or baby showers. Heck, I even considered skipping my younger sister's wedding just to avoid hearing any of the, "So, when are you getting married" bullshit. Other times I've shown up dressed to kill and mentally prepared with sharp comebacks for anyone who dared to ask about my personal life.

Four years ago I was asked to do a segment about "Dating Dos and Don'ts" for single women on *Steven and Chris*. The first segment got so much positive feedback that I became a regular guest, which led me to write this book. After years of research on the topic of relationships, this is what I learned: in pretty much every country and culture there's an unspoken belief that your worth is connected to your ability to find a mate. It's your official passage to adulthood, which is why traditionally your parents give you away at your wedding, and some consider it the most important relationship that you'll ever have. Most societies believe that you aren't complete until you find your "other half." The longer it takes you to find your partner, the more "experts" suggest you lower your expectations and be willing to compromise. That's the polite way of telling single women to settle.

Blogger Natalie Brooke wrote an article for the *Huffington Post* titled, "Getting Married Is Not an Accomplishment."[10] Right off the bat she lets her readers know she's engaged and begs them to hear her out before filling up the comment box with angry responses. She goes on to express her frustration over the fact that proposals are more celebrated than achieving great career success or graduating college, and she is right. Weddings are the only large-scale parties thrown for adults, not to mention they are a billion-dollar industry. The Learning Channel (TLC) has dedicated an entire night of its programming schedule to *Say Yes to the Dress*, a show documenting soon-to-be brides choosing their wedding dresses. Pretty much everywhere you look, married women are being hoisted in the air and celebrated like a Jewish couple during the hora, while single women are relegated to the back of the reception hall, trapped at the dreaded singles table. Oh, the horror!

After reading the article, I began to sympathize with the women I knew who had settled. They just wanted to fit in and be celebrated. Unfortunately for Natalie Brooke, most of her readers did not get it and blew up the Twitterverse with hateful comments. Angry conservative women accused Brooke of diminishing the importance of the institution of marriage. She ended up apologizing and trying to explain her stance on a bunch of morning talk shows.

## Dating Horror Story #5
### Joanne B.

Our date was a blind set-up by my friend Grace. She knew my type, and the guy she connected me with was that type, so she thought we'd hit it off.

She gave him my email address (because that's how it went down in the early aughts), and we exchanged pics, words, witticisms.... There was definitely a connection and a mutual attraction, and so it continued until we decided it was time we met.

I recall that when we were trying to meet, he was flying out of town on Friday that week, so we could either meet Thursday before he left or wait until the following week. We agreed on the Thursday.

The night of our date I remember feeling a sense of ... unease, but I shrugged it off as just jitters and went ahead with our plan to meet at eight. When I showed up he greeted me warmly. He was just as cute in person as he was in his photos. It was a cold, rainy night, so we opted to stay in and watch a movie.

That's when his behaviour started veering off. I can't pinpoint anything in particular, but we watched the movie at opposite ends of the couch, not talking or touching. When it was done, I feigned tiredness and moved to the front hall to get my coat.

That's when I heard him call: "Jooooooooaa-aaaaaaaaaannnnnnnnnnne …"

The hairs on the back of my neck stood up. I slowly walked back to the living room. And that's where I found him, lying on the couch, his track pants down around his knees … masturbating furiously.

I got the hell out of there SO fast.

Again the purpose of this book is to empower single women and to change the awful narrative that we're all pathetic, desperate women looking for anyone to take us off the market. Part of the reason I think some of us settle is so we can be part of the status that's considered "normal," even though no one ever questions the quality of most marriages. A lot of folks still consider a bad relationship way better than no relationship. I may seem idealistic, but my wish is for everyone to be happy and to always be striving for the best for themselves, whether single or married.

So how can you tell if you're settling? Here are 20 signs that you're settling in your relationship:

1. You don't see a future with this person.
2. You're always justifying why you're with them.
3. You're not happy but you're too terrified to end things.
4. You pretend to be happy in public.
5. You've thought a lot about what life would be like with someone else.
6. Your relationship makes you feel trapped.
7. You're always trying to justify their behaviour to others.
8. You talk very negatively about your partner or relationship.
9. You don't like the way your partner treats you, but you do nothing about it.
10. Other couples' happiness bothers you and makes you feel jealous.
11. You can see the expiration date on your relationship.
12. You avoid expressing yourself to avoid fights.
13. You often find yourself fantasizing about other people.
14. You're constantly checking up on your ex to see what they're up to.
15. Everything your partner does irritates you.
16. You often think that you could have done much better.

17. You don't feel like you can be your authentic self around them.
18. You feel empty when you talk about your partner, or you try to avoid talking about them.
19. You'd rather be unhappy than alone.
20. You're scared to start over.

# 10

# INSECURE MUCH?

*"When one feels seen and appreciated in their own essence, one is instantly empowered."*

—Wes Angelozzi

FOR MY JOB, AND IN MY SEARCH FOR TRUE LOVE, I've read just about every relationship book and blog known to human-kind. There's nothing I haven't tried in my quest to find the guy of my dreams. But in my search for answers about how to find true love, I have learned that there's no magical formula, no easy five-step program. In fact, I — or rather we — have "it." What is "it"? By this I mean the answers to finding that wonderful partner we have written about in our journals or pinned to our vision boards. IT begins with the way you see yourself, talk to yourself, and love yourself. My therapist told me if I want to find all the answers about how much I love or hate myself, I should think about the way I talk to myself. When I looked back at my journal entries, I was mortified to read what I wrote about myself. On the outside I project confidence, but I had been clueless about how much I beat myself up. Working in television teaches me how to fake it because the audience doesn't want to listen to a person who seems unsure about herself or doesn't exude confidence about what she's talking about. The harsh reality was that I was constantly picking on myself for not being skinny enough, smart enough, pretty enough, or sexy enough.

Sometimes I would meet couples and afterwards I'd think, how did she get him? She's not that attractive, she doesn't have a great job, or she's overweight, but he clearly loves her. That was not only my ego talking but also my insecurity, questioning how an imperfect woman could find love because I was convinced that I needed to be perfect to be loved. Surely, if I could be the perfect size 4 or have the perfect job then someone great would love me. Sad, right? I don't know where I got this idea. Perhaps it's from all of those romantic comedies I watched in my adolescence, where the regular girl is ignored by the cute guy in school until she gets a makeover and does her hair, and then he notices her and takes her to the prom. No matter where these foolish ideas came from, I wasted a lot of years thinking I wasn't good enough for the guys I really wanted to

date. Deep down I knew I deserved a wonderful partner, but how could I be with an extraordinary guy if I
didn't think I was extraordinary?

Of all the chapters in my book this might be the
most important. Insecurity is a mental assassin that can
dismantle the most perfect relationship before it even
gets started. Even if there were a formula for finding and
keeping the man of your dreams, if you don't think you
deserve love, it won't work no matter what you do.

If you want love and a healthy relationship, you have
to first set that as your intention, believe you deserve
it, and get rid of any negative thoughts that are holding you back from thinking it can happen. According
to therapist Dr. Carol Langlois, "Self-sabotage is your
mind's way of working against you for no logical reason. Basically, it stems from unconscious beliefs that
you are unworthy of happiness, love and/or success."[11]

Be honest with yourself. Are you holding yourself
back? Do you find yourself thinking or saying things like

> "There are no good men left."
>
> "Men my age only want 20-year-old
> girls."
>
> "Guys never notice me when I go out
> with my girlfriends."
>
> "All the good guys are either married
> or gay."

## Dating Horror Story #6
### Tina C.

My boyfriend John* started acting strangely after three years of dating. He would say he was on his way to my place then show up hours later; he never seemed to have money, but he was working full-time; and I thought it was strange that he never bought new clothes. He wore the same clothes for three years. He still lived at home with his parents and had no car. Sounds like a winner, right? I guess love is blind. He was very smart and handsome, so I suppose that kept me interested.

Anyway, one night he said he was going to take the bus — I think it was actually three buses — to come over to my place. Several hours later he still had not shown up. He seemed a bit fragile, so I thought I would get in my car and look for him. I was worried. I didn't really have a plan — I guess I thought I might find him stranded at a bus stop. What was I thinking?!

I had no luck finding him, so I went home and hoped for the best. Another couple of hours later he showed up drunk. I was livid. It was just so ridiculous. He told me he had stopped to have drinks with a friend at some dive bar. I just thought the whole thing was pathetic. After we argued for a bit, I let him stay over because he was in no shape to get home on his own.

The next morning I decided to have "the talk" about ending things. I was just over it. I guess to save face he said that he wanted out too, that he was under a lot of stress. Then he told me that some bookies wanted to break his legs because of a gambling debt. I was shocked! I thought he was crazy and didn't know whether to believe him. I was so fed up, and I didn't know what was true. I asked him to leave, and he had the nerve to ask me for change for the bus! Who does that?! I said no and told him to find his own way home. I really didn't care if he walked. I'm not sure how he got home.

Fast forward to a year later. He called me to say that he made it all up. There was no gambling problem, and he had just been trying to save face, like I thought. I told him that I think even less of him now, and I still think he's crazy!

*Name has been changed.

Listen, as a woman I understand the struggle of dealing with your insecurities. I have stretch marks and cellulite on my butt and thighs; a hammertoe on my right foot; a thick three-inch scar on my abdomen; and dark marks and discolouration on my face from the years of having acne. I could go on, but I think you get the picture. For the most part I don't often think about my imperfections until I start dating someone new; then all of the questions fill my head, what if he sees my scar? Suppose he's into feet? My size-10 hooves and hammertoe are sure to send him running for the hills.

Insecurities can arise from a number of circumstances. Comments from well-meaning relatives or friends might set you off, or perhaps you were teased as a kid, or maybe your verbally abusive ex-boyfriend filled your head with negative feelings about yourself. I once dated a guy who told me that I wasn't very pretty but I was still attractive. What a prick.

My self-doubt wasn't just about my looks. For a long time I thought I had to chase or coerce a guy to like me. If I had a dollar for every time I texted, then double-texted and left cutesy long-winded voice mail messages for guys who really weren't into me, I'd have at least $2,700, for real. By the way, if you're guilty of doing this, stop it. I mean it — stop it right now. I know you really like him, and you're thinking perhaps he didn't get your last 30 text messages, but trust me — he did. And it doesn't matter why he's not calling or texting you back; the fact is that he's not calling.

Self-confidence is the sexiest part of any woman, and as Dr. Langlois says, "Self-sabotage can be reversed. It just takes figuring out the triggers, implementing the proper tools, and consistently changing those negative thought patterns and self-talk."[12]

Knowing what you want and having a strong feeling of self-worth is more valuable than owning any red-bottomed shoe or designer bag. It will also help you cut through all the dating bullshit. A confident woman with her own life, interests, and standards doesn't have time for a man who wants to play games. She knows that if this guy isn't interested in her, another guy will be, so no use hanging around waiting to figure it out.

My low self-esteem kept me boxed in and quiet for a long time. I can remember so many times when I really wanted to say how I felt or to speak up when I didn't like the way things were going, but I kept quiet just so I could be liked. That desire to be liked almost got me raped when I was in high school. My gut was telling me to leave the situation, but I was so concerned about getting this guy to like me that even when he was trying to tear my clothes off, I still couldn't find my voice. Luckily I got away from him without incident, but I learned a valuable lesson that afternoon: set a standard and always speak your mind, especially if you are uncomfortable.

Another important attribute I think all women should have is independence. When I was in my early 20s, I had enough money to buy a house, but I waited because I was sure that my future husband would come along, and we would buy our home together. That never happened. Around the same time my friend Marlon had just broken up with his girlfriend, and when I asked what happened, he told me that she was too dependent on him. When they had first met, she had hobbies, friends, and a life, but as soon as they began dating, he felt she ignored all of those things and just waited around for him. It turned him off completely. His complaint about his ex resonated with me, and I stopped holding myself back from doing things that I wanted to do. I took salsa lessons, learned to play golf, travelled all over the world, and bought a sports car and a condominium.

A woman is more appealing if she creates a life she loves, works on things she's passionate about, and generally has her own thing. Relying on a man to entertain you is not only childish but also very needy. Have you ever heard a guy say, "Man I love a needy woman who doesn't have her own life"? No, me neither.

Everyone has insecurities, even the pretty people. Bringing up what you hate about yourself or trying to hide your true self is a waste of time, not to mention a massive turnoff. There are always going to be people trying to knock you down and insult you, but their opinions are none of your business. They don't matter at all. How you feel about yourself is all that is important. Learn to love every inch of yourself, even the "gross" parts. Your divorce, crooked teeth, muffin top — none of those things really matter. It's all part of what makes you the person you are, and that person is worthy of love.

Perfection is not memorable or interesting. I'd much rather be with a person who is funny, loving, and a joy to be around than a person who is "perfect" — which, by the way, is not even a real thing. Remember Molly Ringwald? Her film characters often got the guy in the end because she was different from all the other girls at school. You set the tone for how people perceive you, so make sure the relationship you have with yourself is healthy. Be comfortable in your own skin, and work on loving yourself more.

# 11

# SEX: TO DO IT OR NOT TO DO IT

IN LIGHT OF THIS NEW NETFLIX-AND-CHILL ERA that we singles are living in, I must discuss everyone's favourite topic: SEX. Whether you're having a lot of it or perhaps not enough, it's a juicy topic that usually divides the room. To do it or not to do it, that's the big question. There's a part of me that doesn't think it matters: if you are a consenting adult with an itch you want scratched, go for it; but there's also a very conservative part that thinks women should take a little more time and do a little more research before having sex with a stranger. I know we are liberated women who have sexual appetites just like the guys do, but are we emotionally equipped to stick and move the way they do as well?

When comedian and author Steve Harvey wrote, *Act Like a Lady, Think Like a Man*, his opinion that women give up "the cookie" too soon caused a huge stir, especially among the 30-plus single female crowd. Harvey's assertion that women make it too easy for men to get into bed with them was heard around the world. He suggested that a woman make a man work to win her heart, and related sex to the benefits you might earn at a new job — three-months' probation until we see what kind of person you are and what your intentions are. The book caught the attention of not only women but also men, who accused Harvey of misleading women into thinking that a 90-day waiting period was a path to a real relationship. Instead they saw it as a way to manipulate men and suffocate spontaneity in a new budding romance.

So who's right? What is a woman to do in an era where premarital sex is as common as breathing? Do men really want a woman who will make them "work for it," as Harvey suggests? Or can a one-night stand turn into a happily ever after? You can easily find evidence of both methods, but the most important question is, what works for you?

Are you the kind of woman who can't imagine waiting 90 minutes — much less 90 days — to have sex with the hot guy you met online? Or are you the type who falls in love after your first orgasm? If I've learned one thing from debating the male psyche at many girls' nights, it's that by the time a woman has had sex with a man three times (three separate sexual encounters), she's catching feelings, no matter how much she tries to play it off. Of course, there are the few to whom this rule doesn't apply, but for the majority of us it's something we can't help. For that reason I agree with Steve. Sex is a helluva drug that can prevent people from seeing the "real" person lying next to them. By taking the time to get to know a person, you arm yourself with key information. What kind of relationship is he looking for?

According to Match.com (2014) 73 percent of singles are willing to kiss on the first date and 35 percent would consider having sex on a first date.

Does he know your first and last name? Is he married? Do you share similar political values? Knowing the answers to these questions might drastically change your mood from hot and heavy to cold and out the door.

Many years ago I dated a horrible human being. We dated long distance for four months, and on my first visit he told me that he had gotten back together with his girlfriend and that I needed to get out of his place. And he told me this at 1:00 a.m. in a nightclub. In the middle of the night, I had to find my way back to his place by myself to grab my stuff from his apartment. I've never been that angry in my life, but at the same time I was relieved because I hadn't had sex with him. It wasn't that I wasn't attracted to him, but I followed my gut instinct to wait until I felt 100 percent about our relationship. I wish I could write that I have always made the right decisions, but that would be a lie. The only reason I had chosen not to screw that douchebag was because of the douchebags I'd slept with before him. Once you've had sex and you're in the company of a person who is kissing all the right spots and saying the filthy things that turn you on, how can you wait 90 days? The answer is simple. Ask yourself what you want.

Holding out for a certain amount of time may give you a sense of control over a situation in which you may be feeling powerless. Turning sex into a cat-and-mouse game is also risky. No one wants to feel like their feelings are being played with. Having a man beg and plead for sex might be fun for a while, but suppose he's on to your game. What if he waits and waits, only to end up leaving later? Then who's in the drivers seat? On the other hand, make sure you aren't suffering from the "fuck and hope syndrome," which is when you have sex with a guy and hope he returns your text message the next day. Honesty, trust, and respect for one another should be a factor in every relationship, regardless of whether it's for a night or a lifetime.

There's a new — or should I say old — dating trend back in vogue. Waiting to have coitus after marriage. Here's the twist: it's not for virgins; it's for people who have already had sex. Singer Ciara, comedian Sherri Shepherd, and actress Meagan Good all publicly announced that they chose not to have sex with their spouses until after their wedding day. I can already hear what you're thinking.

Where are you going to find a man who is willing to wait until the wedding night to have sex? Most aren't willing to wait two weeks! I don't have the answer to that. If you are a born-again Christian or involved in any other type of strict religion, this guy may not be so hard to find, but what about the rest of us heathens? Are we all just riverboat gamblers, hoping lady luck will send us a nice guy to love us, warts and all? I, for one, am not leaving my love life to chance or in the hands of some fool I met at the bar. Instead, I've decided to put on my big-girl panties, use what've I've learned in over 20 years of dating experience, and own all of my decisions. If I haven't figured out how to tell if a guy really likes me, well, then kissing all these frogs has been in vain.

## Dating Horror Story #7
### Charmaine B.

I had a terrific romance dating a sweet, caring, and intelligent guy for two months. We shared so many interests and passions. It was an amazing connection and journey – until I left for vacation for six days. For the first three days I was away, he continued to correspond with me as usual. I got paranoid when he ghosted for the last three days – no contact. My friends told me that I was just trying to find fault in him and not really seeing clearly. They thought he was giving me space until I returned from holiday. He wanted me to enjoy my trip. (C'mon ladies! There's nothing more narcissistic than a guy who wants you to think of him when you are away rather than meeting someone else on vacation.) I returned home, and still, no contact. He knew when I was due home because he had planned to see me. I took a gamble and contacted him.

Something felt different in his tone. I decided to actually ask what happened while I was away because he seemed different. I needed to make some sense of his silence. At least I got the truth: he met someone while I was out of the country. Yep, in three days, he met the woman of his dreams! I took the high road and wished him and his new conquest well – although I didn't put it quite that way. I was very polite. He didn't respond with any maturity or wish me well in return.

Four months later I received a text. He started by saying that this might be an awkward or unwelcome text, but he was wondering if I would be interested in a "hook-up." Not an actual date, with an offer of dinner, a movie, or a sporting activity, BUT a hook-up … Seriously?!

# 12

# WHY DO MEN CHEAT?

THE MOST POPULAR QUESTION I've encountered in all my conversations about relationships is "why do men cheat?" So when I decided to write this book, I knew I had to address this topic. My first boyfriend cheated on me. But before I get into the details of his betrayal, it's important to know he had cheated on every single girlfriend he'd ever had. His father also openly cheated on his mother, and all of his close friends had side chicks. There was probably no chance he was going to be faithful to me, which is something I wish I had known, but most cheaters are also very good liars and are only concerned about themselves. Unfortunately, it's much easier to see the truth and all of the little hints of trouble after the fact.

When my ex, let's call him Schmarc, and I met, I was a 19-year-old virgin who had only dated two other guys. The first year of our relationship was awesome. We never argued, I never felt pressure to have sex, and he always went out of his way to do sweet things for me. The following year was not as picture perfect. He would start silly arguments and accuse me of not trying hard enough. He began asking me to do things like put his car insurance in my name (which I never did). I caught him cheating on a Friday night. He had started another silly argument with me and cancelled the plans we had. Being the sweet girlfriend I was, I decided to go to his apartment with his favourite junk food and bury the hatchet. I had a key, and as I entered his apartment, I heard a woman's voice coming from his bedroom. I walked down the hall and was confronted by Schmarc and his houseguest sprawled out naked on his bed. I was so shocked that I immediately turned around and left. I got halfway down the hallway and turned around, walked back in, and began yelling at him. To my surprise he was not at all apologetic. Instead, he blamed me for not calling before I came over. Remember, this fool had given me a key to his place, but I was supposed to call before I came over? We argued for a while, and then he grabbed my face and shoved me to the floor. As I lay on the floor I remember crying uncontrollably. I was so hurt — not only emotionally but also physically. When I got up, I was so scared he would hit me again that I recoiled as he tried to grab my arm, and then I made a dash for the door. We broke up that night, but he continued to try to contact me for months after that incident. He stalked me and threatened to kill any man who came close to me. One evening I arrived home to find him sitting in the living room, chatting with my parents. I eventually had to change my number and move to get away from him.

For a long time after we broke up I tried to figure out why this had happened to me. Not only was I embarrassed to tell people why we broke up, but I was also scared to talk about the physical abuse. The few people I did tell were as baffled as I was and said stuff like, "You two seemed so good together." I never reported him to the police.

It's a common mistake for women to blame themselves for their partner's infidelity. What does this other woman have that I don't? Is she prettier than me? Is she "a Becky with good hair"? Is she better in bed than I am? Why? Why? Why? The first thing you need to do is stop blaming yourself because it's not your fault. The problem is not with you; it's with him. Every case is different, but here are some possible reasons he cheated on you:

- He's a natural-born liar. He's been lying to you from the beginning of your relationship. He has probably cheated on every woman he's ever dated, which if he's half smart, he'll never admit to you.

It's particularly hard to believe his cheating ways because he's probably said things to you like "I love you," "You're the woman of my dreams," or worse, "Let's get married."

- Of the men who cheat, 56 percent are happy in their relationship but may have become unsatisfied with its current state.[13]

- Most men cheat on their partners with women they know, and 60 percent of affairs start at work.

- He seeks confidence. It's difficult for a lot of men to turn down advances from the opposite sex. It's empowering to be desired, and sex is a great way to top up his ego.

- Men who cheat want it all and think it's possible to have both a girlfriend and a side chick without confronting their real issues.

- He has immature friends. A lot of the research I read suggested that having friends with low moral standards is a contributing factor in a man's decision to cheat. The "bro code" protects them from ever being outed.

- Even after getting caught and ending the affair, men still miss the excitement of the affair.

- He's emotionally damaged. A lot of the baggage we have comes from what we saw at home or from our previous experiences in relationships. If those issues aren't dealt with, the result can be destructive behaviour like drinking, drugs, and sex.

- His expectations are too high. If your guy expects a flawless partner, it's only a matter of time before he becomes disappointed and will use his disappointment to justify cheating.

## Dating Horror Story #8
### Andrea C.

I was very good friends with a man for about a year. We did everything together: shopping, talking on the phone daily, going out for dinner…. Then we decided to take things to the next level and began dating. We mainly hung out at my house because he told me he lived with his widowed father, and we kept our relationship discreet because we were also business colleagues. After about six months I broke off the relationship because he had been playing hot and cold with me, and our friendship was more important to me than a lame relationship.

We continued being friends (although he kept hinting he wanted more) until one day I got a Facebook message from his girlfriend inviting me to his surprise birthday party. Of course, since he had never mentioned her, I had to ask for details, including how long they had been dating. They had been living together for two years. I emailed him and told him I was declining his girlfriend's invitation to his party. Busted!

I told the girlfriend that he and I dated although I'm not sure she believed me. Her biggest concern was that I had ruined her surprise. Hilarious!

# 13

# FEAR OF RELATIONSHIPS

THERE HAVE BEEN TIMES WHEN I'VE WANTED to be in a relationship so badly that I would daydream about a guy I had a crush on and imagine what our make-believe relationship would be like. I'd think about how I want him to dress, the vacations I would plan for us — it's actually quite sad. On the other hand, I've also had a wonderful man standing in front of me doing and saying all the right things, and wanting to be my boyfriend, and my reaction was to run — not because I didn't like him, but out of fear.

DRAKING

A word originated from the rapper Drake – when someone is behaving very emotionally.

It's like agreeing to go bungee jumping with your friends, but when it's time to let go of the ledge, you just can't do it. I admit that when it comes to finding love, fear has often been the one giant hurdle I couldn't get over. Like most fears, it's all in your head, but what if you've been burned in the past by a cheating, physically abusive, or Jekyll-and-Hyde partner? In that case the fear doesn't seem so imaginary, does it? I wish I could give you a beautiful pep talk about how you should just open your arms wide and accept love, but if you've been through some stuff, it's it not that easy.

My very first boyfriend cheated on me, as I explained earlier. Needless to say, I was devastated, not so much about the infidelity but by the fact that someone I trusted with my whole heart was a selfish, mean-spirited, compulsive liar who carried on two full-time relationships. Eventually I got over the relationship, but the fear of having my heart broken plagued me for a long time. I concocted a few canned responses to the ever-present "Why are you still single?" question and became an expert at changing the subject, but the truth was I was afraid to let someone back into my heart. I wasn't sure I could bounce back from another cheating boyfriend or, worse, a cheating husband. After that experience I made two decisions: the first was to never date another Sagittarius — it's funny how one bad relationship will make you hate an entire sign; and the second was to only date emotionally unavailable assholes. My rationale was that I knew exactly what I was getting into and, therefore, couldn't be hurt by his actions. Men of this type also never hid how they felt or what they wanted from me. These relationships may not have been the beautiful unions I was daydreaming about, but they also weren't a big fat lie either.

While most married people are afraid of being single again, some of us singles are afraid of giving up our singlehood. Being single is wonderful! Doing whatever you want whenever you want to — nothing beats that. Some of my personal favourites are finding the food you left in the fridge is still there when you get home, not having to compromise, sleeping diagonally in the bed, never dealing with your partner's mood swings, and not having to pretend to be asleep to avoid having sex when you're not in the mood. Another part of my relationship phobia was letting a new person get to know me. I'm not talking about the surface me — I'm talking about the bad-breath-in-the-morning, clip-my-toenails-on-the-toilet, farting, and head-tie-wearing me. To be loved, you have to let a person see all of you — that means both the best and the worst. My fear was whether, when they saw the worst, they would actually want to stay. A lot of us on the dating scene have perfected putting the best version of ourselves out there. Just scan some online dating profiles and try to find a person willing to admit to their bad habits. You won't! Much like in job interviews, folks lie so they can get a foot in the door. Would your boss have hired you if you had been completely honest in the interview process? The difference is that love is not like your job — you might get away with lying about your computer skills, but you can't have a healthy relationship built on a bunch of malarkey you think the other person wants to hear.

While I was growing up, most of my friends' parents were divorced. My family used to spend Christmas with four other families until one year everyone broke up except my parents, whose own marriage was less than perfect.

More than half of my friends who married in their 20s got divorced. Some realized they never really knew the person they'd said "I do" to; others found the day-to-day stress of being married with children too much. I've seen my fair share of relationships go belly up, and a lot of the people who stayed together had a whole heap of issues that I wouldn't wish on my worst enemy. I heard one of my friends' husbands bragging about his new man cave, the one area in the house that he can be free and get away from his nagging wife. He was talking about the garage. At the time I remember thinking, *Is this what marriage is?* Buying a house in the suburbs so that you can sit between the weed whacker and the minivan just to avoid talking to your spouse? If that were the case, no thank you. Some of us also feel like we dodged a bullet by not marrying our exes and relish in the freedom we had to walk away without losing our house, children, money, or sanity.

## Dating Horror Story #9
### Annie F.

When the tall muscular guy behind the bar at the hot sweaty club unexpectedly flirts back, you seize the moment and go YAAAAASSSSS! But two days later when you're back in your "office" mode and no longer inebriated, going on a date with said hot bartender seems like a really bad idea. At the 30-minute mark of the most awkward coffee date ever, after I mentally admitted to myself that I had not one more minute of small talk left in me (no matter how hot he might be as a one-night stand), I made up a lame excuse to cut the date short, but he insisted on driving me home. I was halfway into my "this was maybe not a great fit" speech, when I suddenly realized I had no idea how to get home. I had just moved two weeks earlier and I rarely drove, so I was completely lost in the residential neighbourhood. He offered to figure it out together, but I chose to jump out of the still-moving car to wander around lost in the dark instead of spending another minute with him.

Perhaps you had the opposite experience. Maybe your parents had an awesome relationship, so you assumed you'd find the same thing, but no one has measured up. My girlfriend Mary's parents used to chastise her all the time as though it were her fault that she couldn't find a guy to marry her. Her mother would say things like, "When I was your age I was already married with two kids. What's the problem?" They just couldn't understand why their beautiful, smart daughter, who grew up in a loving family, was having so much trouble making one of her own. Frankly, neither could Mary. She later told me she was afraid to disappoint her family by bringing home another joker. I know I feel I dodged a bullet by not marrying any of my exes just to appease my family.

You don't need to have your own bad dating story to become fearful of relationships. There are so many horror stories about online dates gone bad! A woman in Seattle was dismembered and thrown in a recycling bin by a man she met online.[14] That's some dark shit. I can't help but think that at some point these two people were madly in love. They probably had cute nicknames for each other and took road trips together like any other couple — except that one of them didn't know the other was a psychotic paranoid murderer. These types of stories (and trust me, there are lots of them!) fed my fear about relationships and became another defence for staying single. Better single than dead, right?

Being perennially single, I've spent many a Friday night couch-surfing and flipping through the TV channels, which is how I started watching *Dateline* on NBC. Personally, I think the show should come with an advisory for singles who would like to get married one day. Every episode seems to be about people who murdered their spouse for insurance money! Sure, I had trust issues before I started watching it, but the show definitely backed up my apprehension about relationships. Side note to my future husband: don't even think about trying to kill me. Just in case you have any ideas, I've left notes all over the place that say you did it.

For a while I hid behind my career. My career is a good reason not to get into a relationship, right? After all, I love my career! Working in television is not really a Monday-to-Friday 9-to-5 type of job, the hours can be long, and if you don't want to do the work, there are thousands of people who would take your spot in a minute. When my relationships weren't going the way I wanted them to, I buried myself in work. I had a five-year plan that included moving to New York City, and I was convinced that, in order to achieve my goals, I didn't have time to let a relationship get in the way. If I were married and my husband wanted to have children, that would derail my entire plan. If I stepped away from my job, would it even be there for me when I went back? I've seen too many of my colleagues lose their spots after having children, and I have worked too hard for that to happen to me.

As it happened, my five-year plan didn't work out the way I wanted it to, and after being laid off, I wondered whether this was what I really wanted. I was chasing a job title only to find my life had no balance. All work and no play really does make Jane a dull girl! And I was using my job as an excuse not to try. I convinced myself that my paycheque was the only reward I needed. I treated myself to anything I wanted — expensive shoes, trips, clothes, cars, jewellery … you name it. But I was really just buying distraction from what I wasn't willing to deal with: my fear of being vulnerable.

At one point I thought maybe I'd never find love, so I did the most logical thing I could think of at the time. I went to see a psychic. A girlfriend of mine was also having man problems, so we went together. When the psychic asked me what I wanted to know, my first question was whether I would ever find my soulmate. She laid her tarot cards out on the table and studied them for a while. Then she smiled at me and said yes. I followed up with a bunch of questions: What's his name? When will I meet him? Will I recognize him right away? She continued to smile at me but never answered any of my questions. Years went by and nothing. I started to believe that I had missed him, or maybe he died, or maybe I was just another sucker, dumb enough to believe some woman dressed like a gypsy could actually predict my future. The latter is the most likely truth. The notion that there's only one guy or girl out there is so misleading and limiting — plus, where is it written that you only get one chance to get it right?

As I've gotten older I've become more set in my ways. I like things done a certain way. Although I like being in a relationship, I'm acutely aware that being in one also means that I have to change. Not everything, but certainly my rigid way of doing things might have to soften a bit. Over time I've developed habits that I hardly even notice, like coming home and not talking for an hour or slipping out of a party without saying goodbye. Again, the freedom to do and say whatever I want was one of my excuses for seldom pursuing anyone who was interested in me. My fears have manifested themselves in a lot of ways. When I went into counselling, I learned that all that fear was restricting me and preventing me from enjoying my relationships. All of my doubts had become self-fulfilling prophecies. If you fear you'll never get married and there's no one out there for you, that is exactly what you will find.

If life were one big game of dodge ball and everyone was equally afraid of getting hit, perhaps we'd treat each other with a bit more care. You'd hope, anyway. In a perfect world we'd all say what we mean and mean what we say. Everyone would gently end one relationship before starting another one, and we'd always consider how our actions would impact our partner before whipping the ball with all our strength at someone's head.

If you don't want to even give love a chance because of a bad experience you had in the past, how is your daydream ever going to become a reality? I had to ask myself whether I wanted to live my life or sit at home and daydream about it. Brick by brick I learned to take down my wall. The first thing my therapist told me to do was forgive — forgive everyone who ever did you wrong or broke your heart. In order to move on, I had to let go of past hurts. Skeptical that this exercise would work, I approached one of my exes via Facebook and told him that I forgave him. I even suggested that maybe we could be friends. I was nervous at first, but afterwards the relief I felt pleasantly surprised me. My therapist also reminded me that nobody is perfect. As soon as I freed myself from the burden of trying to be the perfect girl-friend, another wave of relief washed over me and, sur-prise, surprise, people still stuck around. Changing my attitude not only made me a much happier person; it has also attracted a lot of great people to my life.

# 14

# THE *C* WORD

AS FAR AS I'M CONCERNED, people are way too interested in trying to figure out why someone is still single. Whether they even have a personal connection, the level of interest is often the same. I've heard a variety of comments over the years:

"If she's so great, why is she still single?"

"Thirty-five and never been married. What's wrong with her?"

"She's cute, but something must be up."

There's a common insinuation that there must be something wrong, some sort of red flag. Or worse, maybe she's the *C* word. No, I'm not talking about *that* word. I'm referring to a much more common word that is often used to marginalize single women.

It belongs to a bigger group of words that includes *stupid*, *slut*, and *bitch*.

Men often use this word to describe any woman who shows signs of anxiety, who is a bit overzealous in the beginning of a relationship, or who carves the words *fuck you* on the side of his car after she catches him cheating (that last one may qualify). All jokes aside, the word I'm referring to is CRAZY. Sometimes it's buried in familiar phrases like "Calm down" or "What are you talking about?" Other times it's just blurted out: "You fucking crazy bitch." Regardless of how it's said, my problem with the word is that it's insulting, dismissive, and typically used to describe only a woman's behaviour.

For centuries "female hysteria" was considered a legitimate medical diagnosis. Symptoms of FH include anxiety, irritability, insomnia, and a high sex drive. And by the way, if this were real, everyone including the pope would be guilty of having the dreaded female hysteria. Originally the term *crazy* was used to stigmatize people with mental health issues, but over time it has become a word used to describe a woman having an emotional response to anything. Further, this word is deeply insulting to people with mental health struggles because it reduces them to an insulting blanket label used to cover a wide variety of illnesses, each of which deserves as serious consideration and compassion as any debilitating or fatal physical disease. All the more reason this is a crappy term to use to refer to women who express emotions or who aren't married.

Don't believe me? Think about what happens when singer/songwriter Taylor Swift pens a song about her relationships. How does the media describe her? She's CRAZY. Actress Halle Berry's ex-husband Eric Benét cheats on her, and Berry confesses that she was once beaten so badly by a former boyfriend that she lost part of her hearing. And what does everyone call her? She's CRAZY, too. R&B singer Chris Brown violently attacks his girlfriend Rihanna, is court ordered to stay away from his ex-girlfriend Karrueche Tran for exhibiting violent and threatening behaviour, throws a chair at a TV studio window after a performance, attacks a fan outside of a night club, and regularly rants on his social media accounts. What do people say about him? "Oh, he's got anger issues." I use these examples not to demonize Brown but to show the way society only uses the word "crazy" to describe a woman's behaviour. Women are seen as emotional while men are logical. When a woman is called "crazy," seldom are any facts required. Hearsay or rumours are all that's needed. That's why it's such an effective way to control a woman, make her second-guess herself, or taint her reputation. Labelling a woman as "crazy" also allows an emotionally abusive man to play the victim, shifting any responsibility for his own actions onto the woman. This is also referred to as *gaslighting*, a term borrowed from the famous 1944 Ingrid Bergman film (*Gaslight*), in which Bergman's character's husband convinces her she is going insane so that he can find and steal her murdered aunt's jewels (74-year-old spoiler: he's the murderer!). The term shows up a lot in media today to refer to women being emotionally manipulated to back down from an opinion or to let a man get his way. According to Daphne Rose Kingma, author of *The Men We Never Knew*, "Because of the way boys are socialized, their ability to deal with emotions has been systemically undermined."[15] This could explain why many guys are comfortable ignoring a woman they have fallen out of love/like with. If a man is confronted by a woman who doesn't like his behaviour, the easiest way to shut her down is to drop the C bomb. It's much easier for him to shove an emotion away — as he's been taught to do with emotions he can't punch or sports his way out of — than to confront it head-on.

Anytime I hear a man describe his ex-wife or ex-girlfriend as crazy, I take it as my cue to grab my purse and leave because I know it'll only be a matter of time before he's telling the new woman he's dating about how crazy I am. As my divorced girlfriend once told me, pay attention to those comments because at some point he loved that "crazy" woman, and eagles don't fly with chickens. I've even heard men use the term "crazy girl sex" as a way of justifying to their friends why they continue to sleep with a woman whom they've labelled as crazy.

Consider, though, that a lot of men have very little understanding of women. They may not realize that stigmatizing a woman for expressing the way she feels can have adverse effects on her and everyone she encounters. Many years ago a guy I was dating told me that he was totally stressed out about a big event he had coming up, so I booked him a 60-minute deep-tissue massage at a high-end spa to help him relax. I thought it was a kind gesture, but afterwards he avoided me and told his friends that I was "crazy in love" with him. Instantly, he and his friends labelled me as a crazy girl desperately looking for a husband. My intention was to do something nice for someone I liked, but it turned into a social disaster for me and made me hyper-sensitive about showing any affection to a man I liked at the beginning of a courtship. This kind of misunderstanding and harsh labelling can have a domino effect on future relationships and affects our ability to properly express our needs and emotions.

Sadly, women are just as guilty as the guys of using the dreaded C word to throw shade at other women. I believe it comes from feeling competitive with one another, and from the baseless idea that by tearing another woman down you'll build yourself up. This behaviour is more telling of the person doing the name-calling than it is of the person being maligned.

Perhaps there are places where we need to be a bit more reserved when it comes to expressing our emotions, like at work or in court, but it's unhealthy to hold back emotions. Our relationships with our friends, family, or lovers can't be 100 percent real if we don't feel free to express ourselves. Telling a person how you feel isn't always going to be pretty, and it may make a few people in the room feel uncomfortable, but it's part of life. Learning how to work through all of our feelings can only make us more in tune with ourselves and everyone else.

The next time you hear a single woman's behaviour being described as "crazy," instead of accepting the claim as fact, take a moment to ask the speaker to explain how they came to that conclusion, and whether they think they played any part in the situation. Women can be emotional, but that doesn't make us crazy — it makes us human.

## Dating Horror Story #10
### Jen L.

I met a very nice gentleman at a bar (at least, he presented himself as a "gentleman"), and I accepted a date after hours of fun and easygoing chatting and banter. He also turned out to be the brother of an acquaintance of mine, so I felt trusting enough to go out with him. Each day we corresponded by text or phone; he was handsome and had a fabulous demeanour filled with sparkle and humour. Our correspondence made me more attracted to him each day leading up to the big date. On the first date, he did everything right: opening doors, ordering my food and wine, joking with the server about us being married (and letting me imagine it), and walking me to my favourite ice cream place after dinner. We strolled hand in hand with our ice cream and chatted about his son, our shared interests, and so on. It was a perfect first date. As we walked to the parking lot, he said with excitement that he wanted me to join him at his car because he had a gift for me. Surprised but intrigued, I followed him. He handed me a Loblaw grocery bag containing ten boxes of Jell-O: five strawberry red ones and five lime green. Ummm? Puzzled, I asked what this meant. He said, "Let's go back to your place and fill the tub with Jell-O then slither around in it together!" I laughed at his idea that this would be hilarious, fun, or sexy. Pausing, I said, "My instinct was right – you're too good to be true!" He interpreted my response by imagining I was very into his Jell-O play-date idea – until I got out of the car, thanked him for the evening, and walked away with the bag of Jell-O boxes. He yelled out the car window for me to come back. I yelled back to him that I thought he was quite a charmer and that I'd had a great time. I also thanked him for the gift — I was supposed to make Jell-O shots for an upcoming party, and he saved me from having to buy! It really was too good to be true! We never spoke again.

# 15

# SINGLE GIRL SOLUTIONS

DURING AN INTERVIEW at Sirius XM Radio the host, who was a woman, asked me, "What gives you the authority to talk about relationships and being single?" I laughed, mainly because it wasn't the first time I'd been asked that question by an angry skeptic. I told her, "I'm just like you and every other single woman out there trying to figure it out, going on dates, being harassed by my ex, talking to men I know there's no future with." The only difference is I'm a journalist who has been asked to write or talk about the subject of dating. Over the years I've gathered hundreds of pages of information: lists, polls, scientific research, articles, and pretty much anything you can think of on the topic of being single and dating. When I decided to write this book, I had two purposes. I wanted to help anyone out there who feels alone going through this, and I wanted to help change the narrative about single women.

I'm not a huge fan of the "how to snag the perfect guy" style of article, but I know a lot of us are. I decided to dedicate a section of my book to "Single Girl Solutions" and share all the intel I've gathered over the years. Some of this information is quite helpful! While some of it may seem a little sexist, I've saved you the time and effort of going through all the lifestyle sections. Have a read and see if any of it helps you. Just know that, in the end, no matter what you choose to do, it should come from you. Don't let anyone tell you what they think you should do. Enjoy!

## TOP 5 TIPS FOR ONLINE DATING

1. **Put your best foot forward.** Is that really the best pic you have of your face? If you are out of focus or covered up, don't even think about posting that picture. Also please don't post a photo that includes you and a bunch of other people. Remove your sunglasses, and be sure to add a full-body picture.

2. **Show, don't tell.** In your attempt to impress the folks viewing your profile, keep it short and simple. It's hard to describe every aspect of who you are, so instead of quoting deep philosophers, let your flirting do the talking.

3. **You are not a comedian.** Don't lead with a joke — unless you are actually a comedian! Sure, your friends tell you you're hilarious, but the folks online don't know you or your quirky sense of humour yet. If you want to add a bit of levity, use it sparingly, the way you'd add salt to your meal.

4. **Think about what you're looking for.** Are you looking for your soulmate or just someone to have fun with? Make sure the image you put online matches the fish you want to reel in. Half-naked and sexually suggestive pictures will get you lots of attention, but is it the kind of attention you really want?

5. **Log on every once in a while.** Once you've set up your dating profile, you have to check in. Most online profiles have alerts that let you know when you have a message, wink, or like. Be sure to get back to the men you're interested in talking to. Also be straight with people about what you're looking for.

## NEW RELATIONSHIP
## WARNING SIGNS

Let's be honest, not all of us like being single. Some women can't wait to quit the dating game, find a great partner, and settle down. And I think we can all agree that the honeymoon stage is amazing: the making out, holding hands, butterflies every time you see him, and don't forget the hot, buck-naked sex. I'm getting hot and bothered just thinking about it! For those of us who would like to get married one day, when you do meet a guy and things are going well, you can't help but wonder whether he's "The One."

In the beginning it's easy to look past little flaws and inconsistencies because your brain has literally shut down. I'm being serious. Studies have shown that the intense fairy tale–like process of falling in love actually slows our brains down. There's a reason they say "love is blind." When we're in love, we only see what we want to see.[16] Between the slow brain activity, raging hormones, and hopes that this might be your one and only, it's fair to suggest you might miss a few indicators that the guy is no good. Relationship therapist Janna Comrie has been counselling women for 15 years, so I asked her to break down the red flags women in new relationships should keep an eye out for.

1. **He's your harshest critic.** A man who tries to convince you of who you should be or tries to tell you what's okay and not okay for you is not respecting you in any way. A man I once dated criticized my house, my hair, my jacket, my lunch, my work, my choice of banking institution, and the brand of windshield washer fluid I bought, all in a two-hour period. The relationship didn't last long.

2. **You're more in love with the idea of who he is than who he really is.** We all have potential. But it takes a plan and the desire to achieve the end point to live up to that potential.

3. **He's not a man of his word.** You've heard him lie to his boss, his family, and his friends. He's constantly late, and he makes offers that don't seem to come to fruition. Sometimes he makes excuses (if he's called on something), and sometimes he just pretends he never made the offer.

4. **He's no fun.** A man who can't laugh at himself and the world around him is very difficult to be with. He doesn't handle stress well (he either gets uptight or ignores it), and he often takes things too personally or too seriously. This usually leads to no communication, poor

communication, or your apologizing for the way you're breathing (or some other ridiculous thing).

5. **He shuts down when he doesn't get his way.** We've all heard the expression "If it walks like a duck and quacks like a duck, it's probably a duck." Ladies, if it pitches a fit like a five-year-old ...

6. **He's a little too private. His devices are always locked and he doesn't bring up anything about his personal life.** I've dated a few of these. (What can I say ... I've had to learn too!) Eventually I found out one of them sold guns, one had a pregnant girlfriend, and one had a wife who travelled a lot for business. If you don't know anything about his past or his present, then you don't know anything about how he came to be the person in front of you. You can't even evaluate whether he's being honest or not. Understanding someone's journey is important to understanding who they are. It explains why things are important to him. If you're not privy to any of his background, you don't really know him.

7. **He talks about changing you.** Although you may think you are smart enough to avoid the guy who wants to change who you are, love's blinders can fool even the most savvy dater. Being with a partner who can bring out the best in you is a gift. For example, learning how to be better with your money or being

encouraged to take that course you've been talking about for the last six years is wonderful. But red flags should go up if you find yourself with someone who wants to change your personality or the way you dress.

You shouldn't be making apologies for who you are. If he wants an Instagram model with stiletto nails and hair down to her waist, wearing sexy clothes, behaving obediently, and doing things on his terms only ... but you like your hair short, prefer clothing you can eat carbs in, and like to speak your mind, don't change who you are. The right guy will love you just the way you are.

8. **You feel more insecure since you've been in the relationship.** Your self-worth should in no way be tied to a man's opinion of you or your relationship. Your worth as a person comes from within you. That said, if you feel unsure about yourself because of things your partner says and does, you need to address the issue.

## FIVE DATING DEAL BREAKERS

1. **You're always having to make excuses for him.** No one's perfect, but you should never have to defend his bad behaviour to other people. You know what I'm talking about: "He's really stressed right now," or "You don't know him the way I do."

2. **He treats you with very little or no respect in public or in private.**

3. **He sees your family and friends as beneath him and is always trying to separate you from them.**

4. **He doesn't trust you.** Dating someone who wants to spend every waking moment with you may seem romantic at first, but if your partner never wants to let you out of his sight because he thinks you're cheating on him, it's a red flag.

5. **You're afraid of him or his temper.** Your partner should be your protector, not someone you feel you need to be protected from. Love is not supposed to hurt.

# 16

# REVAMPED

WHEN I BEGAN MY QUEST to work in television, I dreamed about becoming the next Katie Couric, but the universe had a different plan for me. Four years into my television career I landed my first hosting job on a show called *Exchanging Vows*. The premise of the show was that two couples planned their weddings, and whichever pair did a better job won a free honeymoon. (TLC does a newer version of it called *Four Weddings*.) I learned many things on that set. First, I love hosting reality shows; second, some women are more interested in the wedding day and being the centre of attention than they are in marrying their partner; and third, if a fight breaks out between two brides, the director doesn't care what happens to the host as long as they get it on camera. Lucky for me the bride who lost was removed from the set before things got out of hand, but — I'm not gonna lie — my ass was scared.

A few years later I hosted another reality show called *Revamped*. The premise of that show was to help women whose "happily ever after" had fallen apart, leaving them emotionally and physically broken. Our job was to help them revamp their lives. Each woman attended an eight-week boot camp in a beautiful mansion equipped with a personal trainer and a psychologist. When I first got the job, I didn't give much thought to the contestants. It was just another notch on my résumé — that was until I heard each woman's story about the anguish she'd been through at the hands of a man she loved.

One woman told us that her ex-boyfriend used to literally make her sit in the doghouse if she did something he didn't like. In that moment I knew *Revamped* was much more than just another TV gig. I'm sure those women had no idea, but they helped me so much in dealing with my own relationship baggage. Up until then my way of dealing with the hurt I'd been through in my relationships was to shove it deep down and try to forget it. For a long time I thought I was doing great, even though at the time I was only engaging in meaningless short-term relationships with men I didn't give a shit about. The truth was that I was really angry — not just angry at the men who had broken my heart, but also with myself. How could I have been so stupid? Why couldn't I find a nice guy to be with? Why had I put up with so much bullshit? And worse, what made me go back for more? I realize now that all of those experiences were gifts that helped shape me into a loving, forgiving, well-rounded, razor-sharp woman.

Opening those wounds was therapeutic. As I watched these women, who had dealt with far more devastating situations than I had, turn into confident, strong, and happy ladies, I thought it would be nice if all single women who have experienced heartbreak could have the chance to go on an eight-week retreat and work on themselves. The truth is that a lot of people out there hurting people are doing so because they, themselves, are hurting. Whether the damage comes from childhood experiences or an abusive relationship, it's important to get to the root of the problem in order to achieve the happiness we are all looking for.

## Dating Horror Story #11
### Michaela G.

I had been dating a guy for over a month, and though we hadn't talked about being exclusive, we were smitten with each other and with the direction we were headed. We had constant communication and shared passion, and he told me that he had eyes only for me and couldn't wait to see me. On a fine Tuesday afternoon, we each had client luncheons and we made plans to meet at a casual restaurant-bar immediately afterwards. While I was tending to my appointment, I received a text from a close friend who is also online dating – in fact, I set her up on the same website that I was using. My friend sent me a screenshot of an online photo/bio and string of messages she'd received, and she asked me whether this was the fellow that I had described to her – the one who claimed to be "falling" for me and who I was meeting that afternoon. It was. I sent the guy a text to ask how his afternoon was going, and he rambled on about his work lunch and how he could not wait to see me in a short while. I played passive with him a few minutes longer, then I used phrases from my friend's correspondence with him and segued into telling him that I understood he had been corresponding for the last eight minutes with someone else. He actually denied it. Then I said I had proof. He responded, "Oh, you mean the girl who just deleted me a couple of seconds ago!" Yes, that one. I told him sisterhood is stronger than this and that we were done. He tried to redeem himself and grovelled by text at 2:00 a.m. Apparently he lost sleep over his actions …

## REVAMPED BREAKUP TIPS

1. **Let it out, then let it go.** Vent, scream, and cry. If you don't let your emotions out, they'll fester inside, and so will his memory. So allow yourself one last good wallow. Then *stop*. Need some affection? Redirect your attention to something positive that you like to do. Working out is great, not only for getting in shape but for the release of endorphins — it's a great mood booster.

2. **Retrain your heart.** You will truly forget your ex once you see him in a new light. Imagine scenes you'd like to see happen — it's called creative visualization. For example, in your mind's eye (and *only* in your mind's eye) make him walk the plank. That should harmlessly blast away those energy-sapping, venomous emotions.

3. **Write a relationship profit-and-loss statement.** The end of a romance provides a wonderful time to learn about yourself. For example, remind yourself of your ability to really be there for someone in a crunch. Examine the minuses — perhaps you were too trusting of someone who hadn't earned it. Analyze what was right and wrong about your old relationship. It will help you forge a much stronger one next time.

4. **Form a Saturday night club.** Weekends are tough for the newly single. Call friends early in the week to make plans for the weekend. Have a standing

Saturday night date for a movie or inline skating. For the volunteer-minded, Saturday night can be a great time to work at a soup kitchen or crisis hotline plus you'll meet others with big hearts and giving spirits.

5. **Meet a fascinating woman: yourself.** Do the things you've been dying to try or that you had put on hold because he disapproved of them. Enrol in that acting class, research a new career, take that trip.

6. **Beware the rebound hurdle.** Just when you thought it was safe to go out without mascara on, *wham!* You're back in love. Try to see this new man for who he is, not as a cure-all. It's like applying balm to a chapped heart. It's temporarily soothing, but you don't cure lovesickness by replacing the love object. You've got to really be over your ex before you move on. Which brings us to …

7. **Close the door.** Don't fall into yo-yo love. Let it be over. If he keeps calling to say you should give it one more chance, or that he has someone new but wants to stay friends, don't bite. Cut him loose and celebrate the new, improved, won't-settle-for-anything-less-than-a-great-guy you.

# 17

# THE DATING EXPERIMENT

WHILE WORKING ON *STEVEN AND CHRIS* as their lifestyle correspondent, I had another opportunity to work on a show about relationships, but this time I would be the one doling out advice. My executive producer, Rick Matthews, asked me to do something completely different: he wanted me to help three viewers navigate online dating. I told him it sounded like a great idea, but the truth was I was shitting my pants. Not only had I never done this before, but I also hated online dating and wasn't any kind of expert at it. Being a professional, I took the challenge head on. The viewers' names were Brad, Suzan, and Carolina.

Brad was a 31-year-old computer analyst. He stood six foot four and was clean-shaven, with a hockey player's physique, big blue eyes, and short blond hair. He was tired of meeting the wrong girls and was ready to find a nice girl to settle down with. I told him that the "wrong girl" would always be out there no matter where he looked. When it comes to dating in the twenty-first century, we have to use all of the social media and Internet tools that we have available to us. It was time for him to take his dating to the next level and get online if he wasn't already. I told him not to rely solely on the Internet; it is just one of many ways to meet women. Nothing is fool-proof, but men make egregious, unnecessary mistakes online. When outlining his profile he needed to write more about his passions and less (or not at all) about his personal accomplishments or "status." He needed to be mindful of the words he chose, including the grammar and punctuation. Women notice details, and in the fast-paced world of online dating, a woman may be quick to disqualify him for something as simple as not taking the time to reread his profile and present his best self. I had few more rules for Brad: No selfies in the mirror. No pics in front of his sports car. Rather, a photo with his dog or another pet would be appropriate.

Next was Suzan, a 34-year-old line producer who had tried online dating before but with very little success. After tiring of bars and clubs, she was ready to give online dating another chance even though she didn't enjoy the experience the first time around. I reminded her of the many nights she had gone out with her friends to a club, bar, or restaurant hoping to be approached by the right guy. It didn't always happen, but did they stop going out to those places? No, of course not. Online dating is just one tool. It may not work immediately, or ever, but you could go out to bars with friends forever and not have it work out either. The key is diversification. Mixing social events and activities with networking with friends, smartphone apps like Tinder, and Internet dating is optimal. Using those tools while remaining optimistic and open to new introduction options will consistently yield the best dating results. Since Suzan hadn't been online dating for a while, I suggested she get back on it and refresh her look and her profile.

Finally there was Carolina, the spitfire of the group. The 60-something blond bombshell had lots of energy and a fabulous sense of humour. This woman was so dynamic that any guy would be lucky to get a date with her, but online dating was a whole new world for her. She knew exactly what she was looking for, and I advised her to take advantage of online dating sites that targeted people with specific interests. Many of the hundreds of online dating sites are niche sites — for example, www.farmersonly.com, www.golfdate.com, and even www.seacaptaindate.com. Carolina might not have been looking for a site for middle-aged women, but rather one that attracts people of like-minded lifestyles and interests.

I had four weeks to help set up their dating profiles and get the three of them on dates before we went back on the show to discuss their experiences, and I did exactly that. The segment was a hit. Afterwards I had requests from all kinds of people, asking me to help them or their mom find a date online. I was flattered by all the requests, but the truth is that Brad and Suzan were a breeze to set up on dates. Brad went on 27 dates in four weeks. He was so successful that I started telling him I felt like his pimp. Suzan went on six dates, which I think the average single woman would be happy with. Unfortunately, Carolina didn't go on one single date. Not one. It certainly wasn't for a lack of trying. I signed her up on all the dating sites, and when that wasn't working I called my contacts at the top matchmaking services and pleaded for them to help me find Carolina a handsome suitor. All of them came back with apologies. "Sorry, men her age aren't interested in women her age," one matchmaker told me. Even men who were 10 years older than she was said that she was "too old." I couldn't understand what was happening, so I asked a match-maker why it was so difficult to find Carolina a date. She was good-looking, fit, and well-travelled, and she had a wonderful sense of humour. The matchmaker told me that men in their 60s were looking for women in their 40s and that women over 50 have far fewer dating prospects than their male counterparts.

I was shocked. It was devastating to learn how difficult dating is for women over 50. I couldn't help but think about what all the other Carolinas were experiencing — or not experiencing. All of a sudden it was clear to me why women over 40 feel the need to lie about their age. It's not because they're ashamed of their age. Being single is its own issue, but being single and over 40 puts a woman in the invisible category.

People are visually oriented, which is why every online dating site suggests posting a picture of yourself if you want to meet anyone. Appearance plays a huge part in the dating game. Physical fitness, beauty, and youth are qualities more desired in women than experience, career success, or intellect. What mass media tells women about what they are supposed to look like is affecting us. The online dating site OKCupid did a study in 2015 that revealed what men really want is youth. According to OKCupid, "Once a woman passes the age of 22, she becomes exponentially less attractive to men." Of course, for every study like this one, there's another study stating the opposite, that men aged 22 to 29 prefer older women.[17]

Not only does the dating pool shrink as a woman gets older, but she may find herself competing with 20-somethings. A 55-year-old man, even one with thinning hair and a big belly, still has hopes of dating a smoking hot 25-year-old — and if he's rich enough, it could happen. I don't see a lot of successful 55-year-old women driving sports cars with men young enough to be their sons in the passenger seat. Maybe they want to or maybe they don't, but the stigma and judgment about how mature single women should behave marginalizes them. Women are desexualized as they get older.

We all get more apprehensive about dating as we age. From the outside dating looks like a young woman's game, and there may be a bit of truth to that, but older women have something young women don't: they have their shit together. Older women know what they want, and they are not afraid to ask for it. I'm aware that there are a lot of women just like Carolina, who look good and feel good but who have trouble getting noticed, and naturally that has them asking "What am I doing wrong?"

The answer is: nothing. Unless you are still holding on to past hurts, or you stop seeing yourself as a sexy, viable woman, you're doing nothing wrong. Maybe you have convinced yourself that men your age only want to date young girls. Of course, that's somewhat true, but not for every single man. Anyway, the older guy who is still chasing women half his age has a lot of issues. You don't need that! Just remember: you are amazing, you can find love again, and any bad stuff that happened to you in the past is in the past. Try your best to leave it there and live the rest of your life.

# 18

# WHERE ARE ALL THE GOOD MEN HIDING?

I'LL START BY CONFESSING that I do NOT have the answer to this question. If I did, the title of this book would be *Where to Find All the Good Men*. I've been asked the question approximately a million times by single women. This idea that single men check into some secret location is hilarious to me. I hate to burst your bubble, but there's no magic hiding place. The funny thing is that even in big cities like New York, Chicago, and Toronto, with populations in the millions, the single women living in those urban centres seem to have the same complaint: "There are no eligible men here." The numbers make this argument hard to believe.

I think volume might be at play here. If you live in a big city, the obvious observation is that there are people everywhere all the time. That being said, big cities can also be very isolating. Downtown streets are clogged with people hustling to work or the gym or trying to grab a coffee, but very few people are actually interacting with one another. Sure, you may exchange a few pleasantries with a stranger as you hold the door, but folks aren't really TALKING to each other. Ask yourself this: outside of your job, how many men do you meet on a monthly basis? Two? Ten? Maybe twelve? Let's say for argument sake you meet five men per month. That would make it sixty men a year. Of those sixty men, some may be married, gay, too young, or too old, or you simply aren't attracted to them. That might only leave you with eight to ten possible men to date per year. I don't know about you, but I know there have been some years when I didn't meet even five men I was attracted to, much less ten. The amount of dating you're doing (or not doing) could largely be affected by the number of people you encounter on an annual basis.

When I set out to write this book, the last thing I wanted to do was write another "How to Meet Mr. Right" manual full of the "smile more and wear something provocative" type of advice. But I also couldn't ignore the fact that it's hard to understand how you can be surrounded by water and not have a drop to drink. This is part of the single girl's problem. You may not want a husband and two kids in the suburbs, but it would be nice to go out with a man every once in a while. But how can you do that if you aren't meeting men? I can almost hear you asking, "Andrea, what about online dating?" Of course this is a great asset for single people. If you are shy, busy, or back on the dating scene after being in a long-term relationship, dating apps like eharmony, Bumble, and Match are great if you want to dip your toe in the water. Keep in mind these are businesses. So while you're seeing whether you've "still got it," their slick multi-million-dollar marketing tactics and commercials from happy couples are all a ploy to get you to subscribe … for just $59.95 per month. One dating guru even promises to give you the secret to finding your Mr. Right, but first he needs you to pay $299. One matchmaker told me her services to help you meet eligible bachelors can cost anywhere from $2,000 to $30,000 a year. According to Bloomberg technology, some of the more popular dating sites are worth $5 billion — yes, billion with a *B* — thanks to your faith in finding love online.[18]

I'm not saying that online dating doesn't work — obviously, we all know someone who met their spouse online — but it doesn't work for everyone, and the majority of folks meeting online are in their early 20s and 30s.

So what do you do if online dating isn't your thing or if you can't afford to spend 30 grand to find a date? First you're going to have to leave your house, step out of your comfort zone, and talk to more people. If what you just read made you want to close this book and throw it in the garbage, I understand. I feel the same way. After a string of bad first dates, the idea of making small talk with a stranger at a coffee shop hoping he might ask for my number gave me a strong urge to punch myself in the face. As much as I loathe the idea of doing this, I also know that I won't meet anyone sitting in my house complaining to my girlfriends that there aren't any good men out there. Wedding halls are still booked solid from June to August, so a lot of people must be finding love.

Before you head out on the street chatting everyone up, remember, this is like catching fish with a net, not a pole. The point is to be open to talking to new people, not only men you are attracted to. You will run into a few duds, but do not be discouraged. The duds are great target practice, and they serve as great reminders of what you don't want in a partner. Writer Laura Triggs described her panic about not finding love in her hopeless dating days. As she said, "I was catastrophizing. I was a stubborn romantic ... when I was single I met and dated several good men."[19] We carry a lot of expectations to hit the bull's eye with every man we meet. In reality we should expect to fall short a few times and not be too disappointed when we do. Just shake it off and keep moving. Don't beat yourself up and, whatever you do, never settle or compromise out of frustration or hopelessness.

There's also a lot to be said about having an easy-breezy attitude about dating as well. Dating is supposed to be fun, approaching it like a job hunt or a promotion you really want can also be a problem. People can detect desperation from miles away, so bringing up your Big Ben–sized biological clock or the fact that you've preplanned your entire future wedding is a no-no. If you're in the habit of only talking to men who seem like potential husbands and that hasn't worked, perhaps taking a step back and relaxing might serve you better. Let a man pursue you. You're the catch, and don't forget that!

Getting into the habit of talking to more people is an easy first step for some, but if you're like me you might suffer from BRF, or Bitchy Resting Face. I would never tell any woman to smile more, but do open your mouth and talk to people. Men are more intimidated by us than we think, so cutting that tension by saying hello or asking what's up makes engaging with others easier.

Some of us who complain about the shortage of men don't really know what we need in a partner — notice I wrote *need* and not *want*. I *want* a man who is six feet tall, with a muscular build, white teeth, a strong hairline, and a good job. What I *need* is a man who can communicate his feelings, who is trustworthy, affectionate, respectful, and generous, who knows what he wants, and who has a clean driving record. Do you know what you *need* in your partner? If you're looking for a long-term relationship, it's crucial that you know what you need before you even think about going on a date. Have you ever gone grocery shopping without a list when you're really hungry? The result is bags and bags of junk food and crap that looked good at the time, but it's not at all what you actually needed.

To sum it up, there's no magic place for you to find a date or Mr. Right, but you should always be socializing and should stay open to meeting new people. Online dating can be great, but it's not the only way to meet men. Talking to more people will lead to meeting more people, and meeting more people might lead to more dates, and it won't cost you a thing.

# 19

# THE WHOLE KID THING

FOR A LOT OF SINGLE WOMEN this is a very sensitive subject. For some, the thought of never becoming a mother is unbearable, while for others, the mention of pregnancy or the sight of a child throwing a tantrum makes them recoil at the very idea of having children. Personally, I have been on both teams.

When I was five years old, I lived next door to a little girl who was six months younger than I. We would play hopscotch and ride our bikes together, and every so often she would come to my house pushing a miniature stroller with her dolly securely strapped inside. She pushed this thing around the neighbourhood for hours without any explanation. She pretended to feed it, change its diaper, and put it down for naps, and every once in while she'd get stern and reprimand her naked plastic dolly for disobeying her. I never said anything to her, but I thought she had lost her mind. Looking back, it's very clear to me that she was born with a strong maternal instinct, and I was dead inside. I'm kidding — well, sort of. How else can you explain our polar opposite feelings toward even pretend motherhood?

When I was nine years old, my mother sat me down on her bed and gave me "the talk" about sex and where babies came from. The entire conversation was horrifying to me. I remember her telling me a man's penis gets hard and then he inserts it into the woman's vagina. The words *ejaculate* and *ovaries* were tossed about that room like we were discussing simple multiplication and addition. I left her room feeling as though I had just been punished for something, but I had no idea what I'd done wrong. I remember thinking there was no way I was ever having sex if that's the way babies were made. I later changed my mind about the not-having-sex part, but the baby-making was still a firm no. Looking back, I'm grateful that my mom explained everything to me, especially after learning that 99 percent of my friends never had any sex education conversation with their parents when they were growing up.

Skip ahead to high school. My girlfriends and I were sitting around the cafeteria talking about our future goals and what universities or colleges we were applying to. Then we jokingly described what our future husbands would look like. At the time I was obsessed with LL Cool J, and while I was describing our hip hop–themed nuptials, my friend Joanne asked, "How many odd-shaped-head babies are you going to have with your future husband?" Without any hesitation I replied, "None, I don't want to have children." I still knew without a doubt that I did not want to have kids. Some of my girlfriends looked shocked by my admission, and that was the first time I heard a woman say to me, "Oh, you'll change your mind." Since then I've heard that same sentiment about a million times.

When I was 21, my GP noticed something abnormal during my annual Pap smear and sent me for an ultrasound. Two weeks later she called me back to her office and told me that I had uterine fibroids, a non-cancerous tumour that attaches to the walls of the uterus. They are very common among black women, but mine were very small and I had nothing to worry about. I was so relieved that I didn't have cancer or another serious disease that I didn't really care when she mentioned that it could affect my chances of becoming pregnant. I had never planned on having children anyway.

All throughout my 20s and into my early 30s my maternal instincts were still dormant. At the same time the majority of my girlfriends and relatives were all getting married and coming off the pill so they could start their families. Girls' night quickly went from drunken nights at the club to "mommy and me" gab sessions about the relative merits of plastic or glass baby bottles or which grocery store had diapers on sale — not at all how I wanted to spend my Saturday nights. For some of my girlfriends it was easy, like my girlfriend Tanya, who got pregnant the minute she stopped using her contraception. For others it was the beginning of their journey into the world of fertility treatments and having to accept that the dreams they'd had about having a family might not come true. I watched one girlfriend of mine go through three surgeries to try to get rid of the endometriosis that prevented her from conceiving. In the end her doctor told her they had tried everything, but bearing biological children wasn't in the cards for her. She was devastated.

My friend Jacqueline had a hard time as well. Before getting pregnant with her daughter, she had seven miscarriages, some natural and some dilation and curettage, or DNC, as it's more commonly called. After two rounds of IVF treatments, she still couldn't get pregnant. Her doctor gave her a heavy dose of CoQ10 and folic acid because her eggs were older. She also had surgery to "clean out" her cysts, in order to help the fetus "stick" to the uterine wall. When she lost her first girl at 24.5 weeks, she was diagnosed with an incompetent cervix and thereafter got a cerclage stitch each time she was pregnant to help keep the cervix shut and keep the fetus in. She also used progesterone suppositories. After eight weeks of bedrest (two at home and six in hospital), Jacqueline's little girl was born, but the baby had to spend 82 days in the neonatal intensive care unit. Although I empathized with her, everything she was going through was foreign to me and made me even more certain that I didn't want to have kids. There was no way I would have gone through all of that to become a mother.

In 2007 I opted to have a myomectomy, which is the surgical removal of fibroids from the uterus. My once peanut-sized fibroids were now the size of grapefruits and caused me to have excessively heavy menstrual cycles that frequently dropped me to my knees in excruciating pain. During my last pre-op appointment, my doctor told me that she was going to do her best to remove all of the fibroids, but there was a chance that she would have to give me a hysterectomy. For the first time in my life the thought of not being able to have a child of my own bothered me. I don't know if it was that the option might be taken away, but I asked my OB/GYN to do her best to save my uterus. The surgery took seven hours to complete and my rock-star OB saved my uterus. The recovery was awful. She stitched me so tight that I could barely stand up straight. I also got an infection that turned three planned days into a two-week stay at the hospital.

At St. Michael's Hospital, where I had my surgery, the pregnant patients and the gynecological patients are on the same ward. Maybe it was the cocktail of antibiotics I was on, or maybe it was watching countless women waddle in pregnant and leave 36 hours later with a bundle of joy swaddled tightly in their arms, as nervous fathers walked ahead loaded with bags and balloons joyfully announcing "It's a girl," but I wanted to have a baby. I decided while sitting in my hospital bed that it was time for to find a guy, get married, and start my family. I even sat in on one of the breastfeeding classes at the hospital just so I'd be prepared in the future. No cracked nipples for this future mommy.

I was so happy the maternal instincts everyone had been talking about had finally kicked in. I also felt like my OB/GYN had done a great job, and God or the universe was telling me that becoming a mother was in the cards for me after all. Roughly eight weeks after my surgery I began to feel like myself again. I was back at work — no more hospital gowns and slippers for this girl — my appetite was back, and so was my old attitude about not wanting children. I wrote in my journal, "If it happens, it happens, but there will be no tears if it doesn't."

In the spring of 2016 I had my annual ultrasound, and my fibroids were back. Twenty-six percent of women who have had fibroids have subsequent surgery. There weren't as many this time, but the one I had was roughly 15 centimetres long. Almost 10 years after my first surgery here I was back at square one. This time I knew what to expect and what my options were. My eggs, if I had any left, were much older now. I thought about all my friends who had trouble getting pregnant in their

20s, so what were my chances of becoming pregnant at this stage of the game? After a lot of thinking, I asked my doctor for a hysterectomy. I did the research and weighed my options. Plus I wasn't in a relationship, so I didn't have to take into account anyone else's feelings about my decision. I made up my mind, or so I thought.

After a really honest chat with my OB/GYN, she asked me to sleep on it. "You can't reverse this decision," she told me, "and you never know what life has in store for you." Surgery is also really scary, so I decided to put off the hysterectomy for another three years unless my fibroids start to cause other health issues. Either way I truly believe if I'm meant to be a mother, it will happen. If it doesn't, I'm more than okay with that as well. Society has a harsh way of talking to childless women without taking into account that not every woman wants or can have children. Luckily we are now living in a time when a woman can make her own decisions and adopt a child with or without a partner, and technology is there to help those who are reproductively challenged have the babies they dreamed about having since they were little girls themselves. If you are interested in have children in the future but unaware of your own fertility, do not rely on stories about older pop stars like Janet Jackson, Halle Berry, or Madonna having children in their late 40s and 50s. That's not every woman's reality. Instead, on your next visit with your OB/GYN ask for a blood test to see what your fertility levels look like. The test checks your hormone production, including your levels of luteinizing hormone (LH), thyroid stimulating hormone (TSH), follicle stimulating hormone (FSH), anti-Müllerian hormone (AMH), estrogen, prolactin (PRL), and progesterone.[20]

Freezing your eggs is another option for single women who want to beat the clock. This procedure is very expensive, but some companies, like Google, are now offering to pay for the procedure as an extended benefit. Insurance coverage doesn't usually apply to egg freezing, but it may cover some of the costs. The out-of-pocket cost is roughly $17,000, but more than one round may be necessary. If your workplace health benefits don't offer the coverage but you'd still like that peace of mind that you'll have eggs when you're ready, you must do a lot of research. You'll need to find a clinic near you or ask your OB/GYN for a referral. Most fertility specialists will tell you that time is of the essence, and the younger you are when you freeze your eggs the better your chances of getting pregnant.[21]

## FACT

Did you know that, according to the Population Reference Bureau, there has been a decline in fertility rates among young adults in the United States? For the first time in U.S. history fertility rates among women ages 30 to 34 exceeded those of women ages 20 to 24.

As more women become primary breadwinners, fertility decisions are more likely to hinge on women's earnings than they did in previous years.

According to the CDC's National Survey of Family Growth (2006–2007), 7.4 million women have received infertility services. Sixty-five percent of women with infertility issues who sought medical assistance gave birth,[22] and, according to the U.S. Census Bureau Population Survey (2014), 47.6 percent of women between the ages of 15 and 44 have never had children, the highest percentage of childless women recorded since 1976.

## 20

# HANDLE YOUR MONEY, HONEY

ONE OF THE GREAT BENEFITS OF BEING SINGLE is having all of your disposable income to yourself. Whether you're financially well off or living paycheque to paycheque, whatever extra money you have after you pay your bills is yours to spend however you choose. But sometimes all that freedom can lead to bad habits. Are you an emotional spender who splurges on online purchases to fill the void of being unhappy with your life? Or are you the type of woman who yells out "treat yo'self" as you mindlessly spend money on clothes, shoes, socializing, makeup, and mani-pedis without putting away money for a rainy day? Is your closet full of items that still have price tags on them while you have $0 in your savings account? If so, it's time to put down the credit card and start making smarter financial decisions.

I'm not going to tell you to stop buying lattes or to start making your lunch, even though those are cute money-saving tips. Instead I'm going to pass on some real, sound financial advice that will help you become more accountable for your bad spending habits and prepare you for the future. According to Robert Brown, author of *Wealthing Like Rabbits*, "The best thing you can do with the extra money is pay down any consumer debt you are carrying. Start with any high-interest debt, like an outstanding balance on a credit card. Debt repayment offers a guaranteed and usually fantastic rate of return. It also offers peace of mind at a time of year when a lot of people are stressed about money. If you are already debt free, first give yourself a well-deserved pat on the back. Other personal finance options for the extra cash include making a contribution to an RRSP or a TFSA. Others ideas could include making a donation to a charity or a cause of your choice."[23] Also keep in mind that if you have dreams of getting married, buying a home, and starting a family, but you have a mountain of debt, that dream could turn into a nightmare.

## MATCH YOUR SPENDING WITH YOUR SAVINGS

This financial hack is a great way to keep yourself in check when it comes to your spending and saving habits. For every dollar you spend on unnecessary items, you have to deposit the same amount in a savings account. For example, if you spend $160 on a night out with friends, you have to make a contribution of $160 to your savings account by the next day.

## AUTOMATED SAVINGS

Putting away small amounts of money every time you get paid is an effortless way to build your savings account. Ask your banking adviser to set up an automated transaction for anywhere from $25 to $100 to be transferred to a separate account. This is a great way to alleviate any stress or guilt about not saving your money, and the best part is you don't even have to think about it.

## TRY A NO-SPEND DAY

We've all had that experience of withdrawing, say, $100 from an ATM and wondering where it went. Before you know it all you have left is a $5 bill and some change. Unconscious spending is a pretty hard habit to break, so try choosing one day in the week to spend no money. It will require some planning, but it's not as hard as you think. At the very least it will make you more aware of how you spend money every day.

## 911 FUND

As a single person you need an emergency fund more than anyone else. The economic climate is always changing, and you should be prepared. What if your department has cutbacks or the company you work for files for bankruptcy? It's advisable to have at least six months' worth of income stashed away. You may not find another job right away, so leave yourself enough funds to comfortably look for your next job opportunity.

## GET LIFE INSURANCE

A lot of childless single women don't have life insurance because they figure if they don't have any dependants, they don't need it — wrong. If you die or become unable to work and you don't have life insurance, your family will be responsible for paying off all of your debt. That includes your car payments, mortgage, student loans, credit cards, and any other outstanding debt. According to experts, your life insurance policy should be for six to ten times your annual salary.[24]

# 21

# SINGLE FOR THE HOLIDAYS

THE HOLIDAYS CAN BE A VERY STRESSFUL TIME of the year regardless of your relationship status, but if you're single, perhaps the thought of having to face all of your annoying relatives — who are sure to be asking the standard mundane questions like "Are you dating anyone?" — has you wishing you could skip the entire holiday season. Don't fret; you'll get through it.

Pessimism comes naturally to me. My grandmother was a pessimist, and she passed it down to my mother, who passed the cynical attitude down to lucky ol' me. Whenever I hear someone say "Look on the bright side," my eyes automatically start to roll. Plus experience has taught me that the holiday dinner table, surrounded by nosey, unfiltered relatives stuffed to the brim with food and wine, is a treacherous place for a single girl. At any moment the focus of the conversation might shift to your perennial single status, and no matter what you say, you know they will never back off until you bring a date.

On the subject of holiday dates, there's also that whole question of to invite or not to invite. If you've started seeing someone just before the holidays, it's wise to keep an open mind about the family dinner thing. For some folks it's a big deal to bring a date to meet your entire family, or perhaps you don't want to get your family's hopes up if you're not sure yourself where things are going. Whatever you decide, be sure to discuss what your plans are with the person you're seeing, to avoid any confusion. And if you do invite your new boyfriend or girlfriend to your family's house for the holidays, be sure to give them a heads-up about what to expect. No one wants to be thrown to the lions without at least a warning.

This advice also extends to the work Christmas party. These days many companies don't allow their employees to bring dates, so don't be upset if you don't get an invitation from the person you're dating. If you feel serious about your guy, you can make that clear when you introduce him to people, but if you're the date and he introduces you as a "friend," don't lose your shit. Smile and be polite. Whatever you do, don't make a scene at the party. You'll want to have the discussion about where the relationship is going later, but the party is not the place.

There are a lot of ways to look at being single during the holidays, and they're not all bad. Instead of dreading the holidays, I've found a way to celebrate being single. 'Tis the season to drink and be merry! For one thing, you're going to save yourself a ton of money not having to buy a present, not to mention the stress of trying to figure out what to get him. Instead, invest that extra bit of cash. Robert Brown, author of *Wealthing Like Rabbits*, suggests, "If you are debt free it's okay to treat yourself."[25]

If you're in a new budding romance, talk about the gift situation. It can be really tricky to figure out whether you should buy a gift, and even trickier to know how much you should spend. The answer is simple: talk about it. This eliminates any confusion and lets you know how invested that person is in you.

Emotional drinking and eating was my holiday drug of choice for years. Let's be honest — there's no better time to eat your face off. Everywhere you turn there are sugar cookies, smoked ham, devilled eggs, rum punch, eggnog, cake, turkey legs, casseroles, cornbread, short ribs, sweet potato pie, and cheesecake to be consumed at the endless Christmas soirees you'll be invited to. Try your best not to overindulge. If you can only handle two glasses of wine, have only two glasses. No sense in drowning your sorrows in booze only to become the hot topic at the water cooler after the office party.

The holiday blues can be tough on single people. Try not to let them affect your attitude about your dating future. The holidays are a wonderful time to take stock and review the previous 11 months. And try to take a more optimistic view of your life around the holidays; it's a great time of year to get together with friends and family and celebrate your year. Whether it was good or bad, you've made it. The holidays can be a very stressful time anyway, so don't add any anxiety about being single to your holiday cheer.

## DATING TIPS FOR THE NEW YEAR

**1. Be fabulous.** Whenever you're stepping out on a first date you want to look and feel your best, so if that means dropping the 10 pounds you gained over the holidays, then do it, no excuses. If those extra 10 pounds make you feel good, keep 'em! When it comes to weight management, you do what makes you feel fab. A huge part of attracting someone is putting out positive vibes, and when you feel good, you put out positive energy.

**2. Work on you first.** Looking for someone to come into your life and save you is a BAD idea. If you're looking for someone to help you carry all the baggage you've collected from your past relationships, you're putting a lot of pressure on that person to make you happy. Take the time to recognize the issues that have blocked you from having success in love in the past. It could mean forgiving, finding closure, or maybe even going to therapy.

**3. Keep it light.** You may have written "Get engaged" on your to-do list, but make sure you don't put too much pressure on everyone you meet to be "The One." Keep it easy-breezy, take your time, and really get to know the person or people you're dating. Remind yourself that it's just a date, and that you don't have to marry this guy.

**4. Be the person you'd like to date.** Too often, women are more interested in "marrying it" than "becoming it." Write down all the characteristics you'd like in a partner, and then ask yourself whether you are any of those things. Be honest. When we become the person we'd like to date, we love ourselves more. That self-love will attract the right kind of person into your life.

**5. Scrap your "type."** If you've been waiting for a Shemar Moore type to knock on your door and propose (complete with caramel skin and six-pack abs!), but it's been 20 years and no one resembling that description has shown up, it may be time to reassess your type. Be open-minded when it comes to looks, and focus more on attributes like patience, kindness, generosity, a sense of humour, and common interests.

**6. Make a move.** Stop playing games. If you like a guy, don't be afraid to make a move. I'm all for men making the first move, but realistically the majority of them are just as scared of rejection as we are. Go ahead and start a chain of friendly emails or texts, and see how he responds.

**7. Leave last year in the past.** Still sensitive after a bad breakup, or reeling from a string of awful dates last year? Stop moping and making excuses. Issues are boring, and they make us feel inadequate and helpless. A new relationship means a new start, right? Have fun and give each new date a clean slate.

**8. Don't waste time in an unhappy relationship.** Life really is too short to be miserable. You may be scared of change and scared of being single, but aren't those momentary blips better than being unhappy in a relationship that you know isn't right?

## 22

# IT'S NOT ONLY THE GUYS' FAULT

WHEN I DECIDED TO WRITE THIS BOOK, I wanted to make single women feel valued and to let them know that they aren't alone out there struggling with how society views them. I've spent years talking about relationships and single life on television, and I wanted to put everything I've learned into one fun book that single women could enjoy while sipping on their favourite beverage (personally, I enjoy a glass of rosé). As I was writing, I struggled with whether to include the men's point of view. I'm a journalist, so providing both sides of the story is important to me, but I didn't want it to come off as a "how to get and keep a man," but more of a compilation of what single men have to say about their experiences, and their likes and dislikes. As a savvy businessperson will tell you, you have to know what your target audience is looking for. In order for us to have the relationships we desire, I think we should at least hear some of what the "other side" has to say.

There's no guide for how a relationship (or life!) is supposed work, so it's hard to know if we are making mistakes. There's a lot of trial and error. You could ask your ex about what they did or didn't like, but honestly, who the hell wants to do that? Not me. If you're not lucky enough to have a male friend with a high emotional IQ in your life with whom you can talk about your relationship, then you do what most women end up doing: talk to your girlfriend. There's nothing wrong with having a good vent session on the phone with your bestie, but it's kind of like the blind leading the blind. How many times have you heard girlfriends say stuff like this:

"You're just too good for him!"

"He's intimidated by you."

"Guys don't know what they want."

I don't want to be a Debbie Downer, but this is rubbish. These are the standard responses women have learned to tell their girlfriends after a bad breakup to make her feel like it wasn't her fault. The truth is that she too played a part in the demise of her relationship — we all do, regardless of what went down. Anyway, if you're planning to marry a man, perhaps you should hear his side of things.

## SAY WHAT YOU MEAN

Raise your hand if you are passive-aggressive. Apparently this is a deal breaker for guys as well. If your boyfriend did or said something that you didn't like, but instead of speaking your mind you sulked or, worse, said you were fine, you might be passive-aggressive. This is a major no-no. Holding back how you feel only to implode later on is a horrible way to communicate with your significant other. Communication is the key to any healthy adult relationship, so make sure you're not choking down your feelings, because he can sense it. Get out of the habit of saying things you don't mean. Say what you mean, and mean what you say.

## PLAY FAIR

Chivalry is very important. That being said, men are hyper-aware of ladies with a princess complex. They'll notice if you always expect them to come to your side of town, pick you up, open your door, pay the bill, drop you off, and call the next day without your lifting a finger. This also extends to disagreements. If you pick fights, cry to get your own way, withhold sex as punishment, or strike out because you know he can't hit you back — cut it out. Be fair and reciprocate kindness.

## DON'T TRY TO CHANGE HIM

What you see is what you get. At least, that's how most men want to be treated. Trying to change the way a man dresses, what he reads, whom he hangs out with, what he likes to eat, or how he cuts his hair is insulting. It's important to bring out the best in your partner, but you should also accept him for who he is. So stop trying to turn him into your version of the "perfect boyfriend." You should like and accept one another for who you are.

## ULTIMATUMS

Nothing turns a man off more than a woman who gives him an ultimatum. Not only are ultimatums ineffective, but they make men feel cornered and take all the fun out of courtship. Couples in healthy, happy relationships don't need to force their partners into doing things. If you are clear about what you want from the beginning and you regularly communicate your needs to your partner, ultimatums are unnecessary. It's when communication breaks down, when we feel our needs or desires aren't being met, or when the relationship isn't going in the direction or at the speed we had hoped that ultimatums are usually issued. Not only is an ultimatum a turnoff, but it's a risky tactic that usually backfires.

## HE DOESN'T SENSE THAT
## YOU'RE IN HIS CORNER

If you've been single for a while it takes a bit of time to get used to gelling with another person. You've been your own cheerleader for a while, so paying attention to and supporting your man may not be second nature to you. Men generally place a high value on loyalty; they like to feel that no matter what they're going through, you've got their back. Miss Independent sometimes neglects that cheerleading role, so if you've lost that loving feeling, it could be because he feels you weren't the loyal partner he needed during important times.

## INCOMPATIBILITY

Sexual attraction is a helluva drug. The problem is that, over time, compatibility (or a lack of compatibility) will override those hot and heavy feelings. You may be able to go for a few months without noticing that you have absolutely nothing in common with your new love, but the inability to find common ground will eventually become a problem. For example, maybe you like to shop and he likes to be fiscally conservative. Or perhaps you have different views about religion or politics.

## ARE YOU A DEBBIE DOWNER?

Constantly complaining about your life is something

you might do subconsciously. If every time you see your partner, you have something negative to say about the weather, your co-workers, or the neighbour's barking dog, he will start to associate you with bad news. And who wants to be around a complainer? Life is hard enough! So when you get together with your significant other, try not to be a dark cloud of sadness. No one is asking you to be a chipper happy weirdo all the time, but be aware of the crap coming out of your mouth.

## YOU'RE MORE MOM THAN LOVER

Taking care of your man is an attribute a lot of women are proud to claim. He loves your cooking, you wash and fold his shirts just the way he likes, and you're a pro at keeping his life organized. These are all wonderful things to do for your partner, but be careful: he may start to see you as more of a mother than his lover. A lot of women may feel differently about this subject because in many cultures girls are taught to take care of a man in preparation for marriage. Even in the twenty-first century things haven't changed all that much when it comes to gender roles in relationships. Just ensure you aren't presenting yourself as a replacement for his mommy. A real man is looking for a partner in crime, not someone to tuck him into bed at night.

## TEN BIG MISCONCEPTIONS
## WOMEN HAVE ABOUT MEN

1. If he likes me, he'll come over and talk to me.

2. All the good men are married or gay.

3. If I don't have sex with him right away, he won't like me.

4. Men don't like commitment.

5. All men are liars.

6. Men don't like aggressive women.

7. Hot guys only want hot girls.

8. Men move on from relationships much faster than women.

9. If a man doesn't make a move on the first date, he's probably gay.

10. Men are intimidated by successful women.

# CONCLUSION (THANK YOU, CHELSEA HANDLER)

I'm in love with Chelsea Handler — not in a romantic way, but I consider her my hero. We are the same age and we work in the same industry, but beyond that we have little in common except, of course, our single status. I'm in awe of the way she wields her singledom as a badge of honour instead of being ashamed the way many other female celebrities do. The comedian and talk-show host jokes that her rules for dating work because she's still single. Handler is also very open about the fact that she likes to pursue men instead of being pursued. As she said on her Netflix talk show, "If I fucking like you, you're going to hear about it" (June 24, 2016).

The fearless way she expresses her support for one-night stands and regularly makes fun of marriage and parenting in funny skits on her self-titled Netflix show is refreshing. Not since *The Mary Tyler Moore Show* has there been such a strong, successful, single woman on television who unapologetically embraces being single. But she's aware of the fact that not everyone shares her enthusiasm. As she says, "When you're forty, people start to feel sad for you ... I mean, no one's celebrating the fact that I'm single ... hashtag great time." But none of that bothers her, and she's not in any rush to run in slow motion toward her soulmate. "I'll find someone when I'm ready to find them," she says.[26]

The New Jersey native also isn't afraid to name the high-profile men she's slept with, most notably rapper 50 Cent, and regularly posts nude photos of herself on Instagram — something it's hard to imagine Mary Tyler Moore doing, had the technology existed back in the day.

As a single woman I look up to Chelsea and wish all single ladies could feel as confident as she does. That's what inspired me to write this book. Single women are not lonely and sad, and it's time for that old idea to be buried along with all the other outdated theories, like "a woman's place is in the kitchen" and "women aren't as capable as men." Times are changing, dating is changing, and women are at the forefront of a lot of it. Marriage is a lot of work, and you need to show up as a whole person if you want your marriage to be successful. Men today are not princes but real people with flaws, and your happily ever after may involve not only matrimony but also other great achievements, like becoming a neuro-scientist, real estate mogul, the owner of a food truck, or whatever dream you have. The sky's the limit.

In conclusion, if you're a single woman, I hope this book made you realize how wonderful you are and reminded you never to allow anyone to make you feel less than that. Being single is not a problem. You are enough.

# NOTES

1. Jennifer Aniston, "For the Record," *HuffPost* (July 12, 2016). Retrieved from www.huffingtonpost.com/entry/for-the-record_us_57855586e4b03fc3ee4e626f.
2. Michael Paterniti, "Brad Pitt Talks Divorce, Quitting Drinking, and Becoming a Better Man," *GQ* (May 3, 2017). Retrieved from www.gq.com/story/brad-pitt-gq-style-cover-story.
3. Tobias Greitmeyer, "Stress of Singlehood: Marital Status, Domain Specific Stress and Anxiety in a National U.S. Sample," *European Journal of Social Psychology* (April 2009).
4. Office of National Statistics, "Statistics Bulletin: Families and Households" (2015): Chapter 10.

5.  Victoria Wellman, "Are Our Girls Suffering from 'Princess Syndrome'?" *Daily Mail Online*, (December 23, 2011). Retrieved from www.dailymail.co.uk/femail/article-2077635/Princess-Syndrome-Disney-heroines-teach-trade-looks-value-material-things.html.

6.  United Status Census Bureau, "America's Families and Living Arrangements" (July 30, 2014).

7.  Katie Englehart, "Online Dating and the Search for True Love — Or Loves," *Maclean's* (January 30, 2013).

8.  Belinda Luscombe, "Why Aren't You Married?" *Time* (September 24, 2014).

9.  Zhana Vrangalova, "U.S. Casual Sex on the Rise in America," *Psychology Today* (April 25, 2014).

10. Natalie Brooke, "Getting Married Is Not an Accomplishment," *HuffPost* (February 9, 2017). Retrieved from www.huffingtonpost.com/natalie-brooke/getting-married-is-not-an-accomplishment_b_9189828.html.

11. Carol Langlois, "Self-Sabotage: The Biggest Enemy of Healthy Self-Esteem," Dr. Carol (March 20, 2011). Retrieved from dr-carol.com/2011/03/20/self-sabotage-the-ways-to-defeat-it/.

12. Carol Langlois, "Self-Sabotage: The Biggest Enemy of Healthy Self-Esteem," Dr. Carol (March 20, 2011). Retrieved from dr-carol.com/2011/03/20/self-sabotage-the-ways-to-defeat-it/.

13. Robert Weiss, "The 10 Reasons Why Men Cheat," *Psychology Today* (October 30, 2013).

14. "Mom Was Dismembered in Own Home After Online Date," *New York Post* (April 13, 2016).

15. Daphne Rose Kingma, *The Men We Never Knew*, Conari Press, 112.

16. Loyola University Health System, "What Falling in Love Does to Your Heart and Brain," *Science Daily* (February 6, 2014).

17. Lisa Wade, "OK Cupid Data on Sex, Desirability, and Age," The Society Pages (July 3, 2015). Retrieved from thesocietypages.org/socimages/2015/07/03/ok-cupid-data-on-sex-desirability-and-age/.

18. Alyson Shontell, "Bloomberg Says Dating App Tinder Is Worth $5 Billion," *Tech Insider* (April 11, 2014).

19. Laura Trigg, "How I Found My Husband When I Let Go of My Dream Guy," Verilymag.com (May 17, 2016).

20. Baby Center Medical Advisory Board, "Pinpointing a Fertility Problem," Baby Center (April 2017). Retrieved from www.babycenter.com/0_pinpointing-a-fertility-problem_3536.bc.

21. Kim Conte, "Freezing Your Eggs: 5 Things You Need to Know," Parents.com (n.d.). Retrieved from www.parents.com/getting-pregnant/age/timing/freezing-eggs-your-need-to-know-guide.

ANDREA BAIN

22. William M. Mercer, Inc., *Infertility as a Covered Benefit* (1997).
23. Robert Brown, *Wealthing Like Rabbits*, Ajax, ON: Redford Enterprises (2014).
24. Lynn Andriani, "Single Women and Money — Finance Advice for Singles," Oprah.com (n.d.). Retrieved from www.oprah.com/money/single-women-and-money-finance-advice-for-singles.
25. Robert Brown, *Wealthing Like Rabbits*, Ajax, ON: Redford Enterprises (2014).
26. Melanie Dostis, "Chelsea Opens Up About Love Life," *New York Daily News* (February 16, 2016). Retrieved from www.nydailynews.com/entertainment/gossip/chelsea-handler-opens-love-live-article-1.2532937.